Endorsements

"When a man has passionately loved the Lord and His Word and has dedicated his life to serving Him for decades, I am interested to hear what he has learned. This book is the heartbeat and passion of such a man tied to a lifetime of ministry. I found this book to be very practical in today's culture and I highly recommend it. I applaud LaMarr for his insightful study and boldness to present Biblical truth in a day when truth is challenged on every corner."

Greg Shipe
Senior Pastor, First Baptist
Church, Bellefonte, PA

"God provides! Included in that all inclusive statement is that God provides the freedom to choose. Choices in life always have consequences. Our choices will determine our consequences on earth and in eternity. Pastor LaMarr Pirkle shares scriptural based truths to make the right choices. The Christian walk is a process of drawing nearer to Jesus Christ to reflect His likeness in our words, deeds and decisions. This book provides the road signs and directions that allow us to reach that destination. Just as a street light can illuminate the road ahead, Pastor Pirkle's work can shed scriptural light to navigate some of life's most important choices."

Glenn "GT" Thompson
Member of Congress

We Manufacture Our Own Problems

100% of the Time

W. LaMarr Pirkle

WestBow Press books may be ordered through booksellers or by contacting:

WestBow Press
A Division of Thomas Nelson & Zondervan
1663 Liberty Drive
Bloomington, IN 47403
www.westbowpress.com
1 (866) 928-1240

ISBN: 978-1-9736-4968-7 (sc)
ISBN: 978-1-9736-4969-4 (hc)
ISBN: 978-1-9736-4967-0 (e)

Library of Congress Control Number: 2018914934

Print information available on the last page.

WestBow Press rev. date: 01/14/2019

All Scripture quotations in this book, except one which is noted below are from the New King James Version.

Mother's Translation of the Bible

> There is a story about four clergymen who were discussing the merits of the various translations of the Bible. One liked the **King James Version** best because of its simple, beautiful English.
>
> Another liked the **American Revised Version** best because it is more literal and comes nearer the original Hebrew and Greek.
>
> Still another liked **Moffatt's translation** best because of its up-to-date vocabulary. The fourth minister was silent. When asked to express his opinion, he replied, "I like my **Mother's translation** best." The other three expressed surprise. They did not know that his mother had translated the Bible. "Yes, she did," he replied, "She translated it into life, and it was the most convincing translation I ever saw.

Contents

Dedication

I wish to dedicate this book to the Glory and Honor of our Eternal God and Savior, Jesus Christ.

★ ★ ★

Also, I would like to thank God for the support of my wife during these past remarkable 'Fifty Years' of marriage, along with our very precious son and daughter, who have provided us with six wonderful grandchildren.

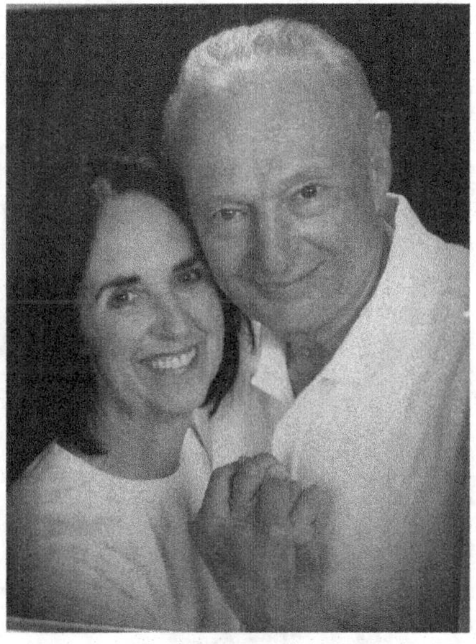

Introduction

Ever since I was a child, there was built within me a respect and admiration toward older adults that were wise and who inspired others with their wisdom.

Once someone asked me, what one person did I feel had contributed the most or had the greatest impact upon my life. At which I replied, "If I were to answer you properly and truthfully, I would have to begin by writing the names in a notebook starting with my mother, family, Sunday school teachers, pastors, neighbors, school teachers, coaches, friends, military leaders, college professors, and the list continues. However, the Bible, God's Holy Word, has had the most powerful influence in my life. Therefore, it is my desire to introduce this book, as one in which will hopefully provide the reader with three thoughts: (1) where you started, (2) where are you presently and (3) where are you projecting to finish? From birth to the grave, we are either projecting to reach goals and anticipating a brighter future, or wasting the life God has given us. If we travel the road to failure, we tend to make excuses in order to better substantiate why we failed. A man can fail many times and still succeed, but he isn't a failure until he blames something or somebody else for a failed life. We are all manufacturers......some make good, others make trouble, and still others make excuses. In defining the noun form of ***Excuse, It is a reason or explanation put forward to defend or justify a fault or offense.***

Billy Sunday said, "An excuse is a skin of a reason stuffed with a lie".

An old proverb....... "Don't do what you'll have to find an excuse for."

Robert Brault said, "There are no such things as a list of reasons. There is either one sufficient reason or a list of excuses."

Have you ever heard someone say, "The Devil made me do it" (made popular by Flip Wilson), or perhaps other excuses such as… 'If I would have been born in a different era of time', or 'If I had lived in a different geographical location', or 'If I had married a different person', or 'had chosen a different career field', and etc.

Marcus Stroup said, "There aren't nearly enough crutches in the world for all the lame excuses."

We are wise to eliminate excuses, stop the "Blame Game" and allow God's Word to assist us in making good choices.

God's Word provides mankind with the pure truth for structuring our lives. God has given us freedom to make choices. Good choices are easier to decide on, when children are raised by sound Christian parents (a few Scripture references – Proverbs 13:24, 22:6, 29:17; Deut. 4:9, 6:6-9).

God not only gives us choices, but the consequence of each one. He has given us the perfect freedom to choose. The rest is up to us. If God removed all bad choices from us, we would have no freedom at all. We would be nothing but robots. God created us with the freedom of choice. Therefore, when we refuse to read God's Word or reject His guidance, we may be likened to one to whom buys something in a box that needs to be assembled, and who fails to read the instruction manual prior to assembling the item. Always remember that the **B-I-B-L-E** should be known as, "Basic Instructions Before Leaving Earth".

In defining the verb form of…. **Manufacture**, (in terms of thinking) it is to concoct, create, devise, fabricate or formulate, theorize, speculate or suppose in our minds, something that is not necessarily factual or real. The only way to discern between truth and error is to compare it to the absolute truth in God's Word.

Problem, defined – a source of perplexity, distress, or vexation. Thus, many varied problems exist, such as: Racism, sexism, financial, health, and family. This can cause us to worry or fret.

It is my desire and prayer, as you read this book, God will allow you, the reader, to fix your eyes upon the only true Sovereign God, who He and He alone, can make your life worth living.

Man has always created trouble, just as seen in the Garden of Eden. A few road signs that could prove valuable, along life's highway, and not be disregarded, are as follows:

- There is only one true God
- Everything He created was good
- God is The Infallible Truth
- Satan is a Liar and the father of all Liars
- There is a Heaven to gain and a Hell to shun
- God is the author of Peace and Salvation
- Christ came and died that we might have life

> **"Men are not sinners because they choose to sin; they choose to sin because they are sinners."**
>
> – Walter J. Chantry

> **"Sin is not just breaking God's laws; it is breaking His heart."**
>
> – Adrian Rogers

> **"Our love for God and our appreciation of His love and forgiveness will be in proportion to the recognition of our sin and unworthiness."**
>
> – Dave Hunt

CHAPTER I

"In the Beginning....God"

> *"Nothing could be more irrational than the idea that something comes from nothing."*
>
> – R. C. Sproul

*****

> *"Darwinism's atheism prevents science from knowing why things are as they are. Without God there is no answer to the WHY for anything."*
>
> – Dave Hunt

If there is no beginning, there can be no end. Therefore, everything has a beginning, as well as each of us. *"Remember the former things of old, For I am God, and there is none like Me, Declaring the end from the beginning, And from ancient times things that are not yet done, Saying, 'My counsel shall stand, And I will do all My pleasure,' Calling a bird of prey from the east, The man who executes My counsel, from a far country. Indeed I have spoken it; I will also bring it to pass, I have purposed it; I will also do it"* (Isa. 46:9-11).

The purpose of the Genesis account is to establish God as Creator. In **Hebrews 1:10**, we read, *"And you, Lord, in the beginning laid the foundation of the earth, and the heavens are the work of Your hands"*. It was never intended to be a scientific explanation of how he accomplished creation. The Bible is not a science textbook. The scientist searches for the **What** and **How** of life's questions, where the Bible addresses the **Who** and **Why** behind those questions.

From the inception of man, he has attempted to psychoanalyze God and therefore, man either worships God or else he attempts to idolize another god and puts himself in the place of God.

Two of the most basic elements of human existence are the uncertainty of life and the fact that death is inevitable. Even for those who think death ends it all, it is only logical to examine what may lie after death and give some serious attention and preparation before it may be forever too late. Someone remarked.... "Eternity is forever and forever is a very long time".

My advice to the self-proclaimed Atheist is read the Gospel of John 1:1-3, which says, *"In the beginning was the Word (Jesus), and the Word was with God, and the Word was God"*. In *Colossians 1:16, "For by Him all things were created that are in heaven and that are on earth, visible and invisible, whether thrones or dominions or principalities or powers. All things were created through Him and for Him"*.

> *"To reverence the impersonal creation instead of the personal God who created us is a perversion designed for escaping moral accountability to the Creator. God indicts those who worship the creation instead of the Creator (Romans 1:18-23); and warns of the corruption of morals and behavior which results."*
>
> – **Dave Hunt**

New Beginnings........

Hebrews 11:3, "By faith we understand that the worlds were framed by the word of God, so that the things which are seen were not made of things which are visible". And looking back at Genesis 1:1, we find this passage simple enough for a young child to understand, while at the same time being sufficiently profound to inspire the greatest theologian. We often pass over such a text so quickly, as Christians, knowing that God is the Creator and we are His creatures that we fail to pause and consider the important teachings or implications.

When we search and study the applicable verses in the Bible, we realize God made everything out of nothing. We see there was nothing else besides Almighty God Himself. We don't read of angels, human beings, or any physical matter. We realize even time itself did not exist, prior to the Creator speaking things into existence. Prior to God's creation, He is self-existent, unlike His creation. However, God depends on nothing outside Himself for His existence. According to Acts 17:28, *"…for in Him we live and move and have our being."* **God is**. *In Exodus 3:14, "And God said to Moses, "I AM WHO I AM." And He said, "Thus you shall say to the children of Israel, 'I AM has sent me to you',"*

There never was a time when He was not, and there never will be a time when He will not be.

The Trinity……

And God said, "Let __Us__ make man in __Our__ image, according to __Our__ likeness" (Genesis 1:26). Then in verse 27, we read – *"So God created man in **His** image". "Our"*…here refers to the Holy Trinity…God the Father, God the Son and God the Holy Spirit. The Trinity is One God, in three divine persons. Although the word Trinity does not appear or exist in Scripture, God's Word speaks about it clearly.

1. There is One God…. (Deuteronomy 6:4; 1st Corinthians 8:4; Galatians 3:20; 1st Timothy 2:5).
2. The Trinity consists of Three Persons… (Genesis1:26, 3:22, 11:7; Isaiah 6:8; 48:16; Matthew 3:16-17; 28:19 & II Cor. 13:14).

Note: There have been many attempts to develop (Illustrations of the Trinity). However, none of the popular illustrations are completely accurate. An infinite God cannot be fully described by a finite illustration.

What Does It Mean, that God is Infinite?

The infinite nature of God simply means that God exists outside of and is not limited by time and space. *Infinite* simply means "without limits." We generally refer to God with terms like Omniscience, Omnipotence, and Omnipresence. **Omniscience** means that God is all-knowing or that He has unlimited knowledge and this is why He is a Sovereign ruler and judge over all things. This is why no one can hide sin from Him. We read in 1 John 3:20, *"...God is greater than our heart, and knows all things."* **Omnipotence** means that God is all-powerful or that He has un-limited power. When answering His disciples' question *"Then who can be saved?" (Matthew 19:25),* Jesus said, *"With men this is impossible, but with God all things are possible" (Matthew 19:26).* **Omnipresence** means that God is always present. There is no place that you could go to escape God's presence. God is not limited by time or space. There are many verses in the Bible that reveal this aspect of God's nature, but one is found in Psalm 139:7-10, *"Where can I go from Thy Spirit? Or where can I flee Thy presence? If I ascend to heaven, Thou art there; If I make my bed in Sheol, behold, Thou art there. If I take the wings of the dawn, if I dwell in the remotest part of the sea, even there Thy hand will lead me, And Thy right hand will lay hold of me."*

This first verse in Genesis reveals that God created time, space and matter on the first day of Creation Week. There is a "faith" aspect of our understanding of God. *"But without faith it is impossible to please Him, for he who comes to God must believe that He is, and that He is a rewarder of those who diligently seek Him" (Hebrews 11:6).*

"In the beginning..." is when time began. There was no "before" God created. God is eternal and He was existing in eternity before He created anything that was created. In Psalm 90:2, we read: *"Before the mountains were brought forth, or ever You had formed the earth and the world, even from everlasting to everlasting, You are God."* God was not created, God is the great **"I AM".** When Moses asked God who shall he say sent him to lead his children out of Egypt's bondage? *God said to Moses, 'I Am Who I Am'. And He said, "Thou shall say to the children of Israel," "I AM has sent me to you" (Exodus 3:14).*

How Did We Get Here

The Bible explains it. In Genesis Chapter 1, we read God created in phases and after each one, God 'saw that it was good'. The Scripture says after He created the heavens and the earth, he created the plant life and all the animals, then He created man.

"So God created man in His own image; in the image of God He created him; male and female He created them" (Genesis 1:27).

On a humorous note in reference to the 'Theory of Evolution' >>> there was an article published in the ever popular "Dear Abby" column several years ago entitled _______

The Monkey's Disgrace

(Evolution – The Monkey's Viewpoint)

The article was actually a poem about three monkeys discussing the topic of man being evolved from monkeys. In essence, they were expressing how disgraceful it was to compare the life of sinful man leaving his wife and sleeping with other women, not caring for his own children and creating problems instead of following God's design for marriage in that He created man in His own image and likeness. According to **Merriam-Webster's** definition of Evolution, it is descent with modification from preexisting species: cumulative inherited change in a population of organisms through time leading to the appearance of new forms: the process by which new species or populations of living things develop from preexisting forms through successive generations, also: the scientific theory explaining the appearance of new species and varieties through the action of various biological mechanisms.

We find such in the study of Darwinism. Charles Darwin (1809 - 1882) provided the theory of evolution in his book entitled, "On the Origin of Species" in 1859.

Note: The last eight lines of the poem best illustrates the humor in the monkey's dialogue ____

"Why, if I put a fence around a coconut tree,
Starvation will force you to steal from me!
Here's another thing a monkey won't do
Go out at night and get in a stew.
Or use a gun or club or knife
To take some other monkey's life.
Yes, man descended, the ornery cuss,
But, brother, he sure didn't descend from us."

– Unknown

Why Were We Created

According to Scripture, none of us are here by accident. If we are willing to accept the Bible as truth, then we know the answer to the question… "Where did we come from?" According to Scripture, we were created by God, but why? He is God, and as God, He certainly doesn't need us for anything – so why did He create us? So that we would accept His plan, which is His Word and follow Him to the level of those mentioned in Revelation 4:11 (the twenty-four elders) saying, *"You are worthy, O Lord, To receive glory and honor and power; For You created all things, And by Your will they exist and were created."*

The average thinking human being is so distracted with non-essentials, as well as ***Noise***, they often fail to understand what life is all about, much less how to live it. This is why the Bible (God's textbook for life) is so important in better understanding the fundamentals of life.

Let's get back to the question….Why did He create us? King David essentially asked the same thing: *"When I consider Your heavens, the work of Your fingers, the moon and the stars, which You have ordained, what is man that You are mindful of him?" (Psalm 8:3-4)* **First,** it wasn't because He needed us: *"God, who made the world and everything in it,* *since He is Lord of heaven and earth, does not dwell in temples made with hands."(Acts17:24-25)* **Second,** God chose to create us anyway, out of His great love: *"I have loved you with an everlasting love" (Jeremiah 31:3).* God loved us before He created us. It may be difficult for us to comprehend such, but that is what "everlasting" means. We read in 1 John 4:8, *"God is love".* He made us so we can enjoy all that He is and all that He has created. **Third,** God created us to carry out His eternal plan. Three scriptures can help us to do this:

1. *"You shall love your God with all your heart, with all your soul and with all your strength" (Deuteronomy 6:5).*
2. *"Love your neighbor as yourself" (Matthew 22:39).*
3. *"For we are His workmanship, created in Christ Jesus for good works, which God prepared beforehand that we should walk in them" (Ephesians 2:10).*

We also play an important part in the war between God and Satan. God's ultimate plan to defeat Satan is mentioned by our putting on the whole armor of God in Ephesians 6:10-18. We can do our part in carrying out God's eternal plan by leading souls to God—through Jesus Christ, His Son. God gives us freedom of choice to do this, if we so will. His Word equips us to carry this out.

In summation, this Scripture caps it off______ *(Isaiah 43:7) "Everyone who is called by My name, whom I have created for My glory, I have formed him, yes, I have made him."*

And it goes on to say in Chapter 43: vs. 10-11, *"You are My witnesses," says the Lord, "And My servant whom I have chosen, that you may know and believe Me, and understand that I am He. Before Me there was no God formed, nor shall there be after Me."*

* * *

During the early 1900s, children's story books commonly began with the phrase... "Once upon a time" and ended with ... "and they lived together happily ever after".

One might say, "And so it is with the Bible" ... "In the beginning God..." and ending with ... "The grace of our Lord Jesus Christ be with you all. Amen."

"Grace" is the most important concept in the Bible, Christianity, and the world. It is most clearly expressed in the promises of God, revealed in Scripture and embodied in Jesus Christ.

Grace is the love of God shown to the unlovely; the peace of God given to the restless; the unmerited favor of God. The message of this grace is proclaimed throughout the Scriptures. Our God is merciful and gracious, slow to anger, and abounding in steadfast love for thousands, forgiving iniquity and sin according to Exodus 34:6-7.

Someone said in the New Testament, grace means God's love in action towards men who merited the opposite of love. Grace means God moving heaven and earth to save sinners who could not save themselves. *"For He made Him who knew no sin to be sin for us, that we might become the righteousness of God in Him" (2 Corinthians 5:21).*

"For by grace you have been saved through faith, and that not of yourselves; it is the gift of God, not of works, lest anyone should boast. For we are His workmanship, created in Christ Jesus for good for good works, which God prepared beforehand that we should walk in them"(Ephesians 5:8-10).

"Grace and peace be multiplied to you in the knowledge of God and of Jesus our Lord" (2 Peter 1:2)

"Grace is free sovereign favor to the ill-deserving." _____B.B. Warfield

Questions for Personal Evaluation or Group Discussion

Chapter 1

1. What is the difference between atheists and agnostics?

2. What two things factor in as to what an atheist perceives?

3. What two scripture passages should be given to a self-proclaimed atheist?

4. How would you describe the Trinity?

Notes

CHAPTER

II

"Marriage"

"Marriage is Symbolic of Christ and the Church"

Marriage: *"If you want something to last forever, you treat it differently. You shield it and protect it. You never abuse it. You don't expose it to the elements. You don't make it common or ordinary. If it ever becomes tarnished, you lovingly polish it until it gleams like new. It becomes special because you have made it so, and it grows more beautiful and precious as time goes by."*

– F. Burton Howard

God Designed Marriage

If anything is designed, it's because there is a designer. It could be a car, an airplane, or a house; it could even be a marriage. There is always a mastermind behind the master plan.

Since marriage was designed by God, we must look into His book, the Bible. Unlike other books which may have hundreds of plans, His only has one. And His plan for marriage is likened unto Christ and the Church (Ephesians 5:22-29). Many couples fall into the trap Satan has set for them by looking in all the wrong places such as: television, movies, magazines and the internet, instead of looking to the master designer to find out what God intended for marriage. If you've tried understanding marriage or love through the eyes of the world, there is a better way.

Prior to building a house, you should have a blueprint. In Genesis 2:18, 21-23, we read, *the Lord God said, "It is not good that man should be alone; I will make him a helper comparable to Him." And the Lord God caused a deep sleep to fall on Adam, and he slept; and He took one of his ribs, and closed up the flesh in its place. Then the rib which the Lord God had taken from man He made into a woman, and He brought her to the man. And Adam said: "This is now bone of my bones and flesh of my flesh; she shall be called Woman, because she was taken out of Man."*

You say, why did God create a second human being from a part of the first? Upon seeing her, perhaps Adam may have observed, "It's me, but not me."

Since the Trinity is a family, then man in God's image must be made a family also. Unlike animals, both relationship and communion are important to this process.

In Genesis 2, we see God created woman from the side of man so that man would not be alone. Comparatively speaking, in the New Testament, God created the church from the second Adam, Christ, for the exact same reason, close fellowship. In Genesis 2:24, we note the Bible says, Adam called her Woman, and for that reason a man is to leave mother and father and be united to his wife to become one flesh. This is so the design of God's image in humans can be revealed.

We must not take *"become one flesh"* literally, but rather in a spiritual comparative significance. In other words, the union of a man and a woman in marriage is not literally recombining two bodies into one, but rather a spiritual mystery such as we are with Christ, just as Christ prayed in John 17. Here He prays for Himself, for His disciples and for all believers. The power of that union is intended to reveal the very image of God to angels and archangels and all those of heaven and earth. This is why Satan fights so desperately to pervert and destroy human sexuality, holy matrimony, the family, and fatherhood in particular.

Therefore, Holy Matrimony is not to be compared on the same level with that of a civil ceremony.

In the scriptural passage of Ephesians 5, Paul uses Genesis 2:24 as his proof reference, which says, *"two becoming one flesh"* for which The MacArthur Study Bible footnote states: "One flesh speaks of a complete unity of parts making a whole." In Ephesians 5:32, Paul speaks of a man and woman becoming one flesh, *"This is a great mystery, but I speak concerning Christ and the church."* He goes on to say in verse 33, *"Nevertheless let each one of you in particular so love his own wife as himself, and let the wife see that she respects her husband."*

God the Master Builder

The American family is crumbling and has been for the past several years. The family structure as we once knew, as husband, wife and children, makes up less than 25% of all marriages in our country. And 60% of all marriages end in divorce and more than 45% of Americans think marriage is either obsolete or has no value.

One primary reason for this way of thinking is people either forgot or do not know that Marriage is God's plan. He designed marriage to meet our deepest emotional, spiritual and physical needs. When He created Adam, God knew … *"it's not good for man to be alone"* (Genesis 2:18). So God brought Eve to Adam and began the first marriage. This is why we read in Hebrews 13:4, *"Marriage is honorable among all, and the bed undefiled; but fornicators and adulterers God will judge."*

We should follow God's original **"Blueprint"** for how marriage and families are designed to work. God changes not and it's His desire for us to not envision marriage as the world sees it.

Even if we come from a dysfunctional family or a dysfunctional past, it is still possible to know how to understand love the way God intended. God's instructions for marriage: (1) Submit to God and each other. Ephesians 5:22-29, *"Wives, submit to your own husbands, as to the*

Lord. For the husband is head of the wife, as also Christ is head of the church; and He is the Savior of the body. Therefore, just as the church is subject to Christ, so let the wives be to their own husbands in everything. Husbands, love your wives, just as Christ also loved the church and gave Himself for her, that He might sanctify and cleanse her with the washing of water by the Word, that He might present her to Himself a glorious church, not having spot or wrinkle or any such thing, but that she should be holy and without blemish. So husbands ought to love their own wives as their own bodies; he who loves his wife loves himself. For no one ever hated his own flesh, but nourishes and cherishes it, just as the Lord does the church." (2) It takes three to make a good marriage – God, the man and the woman. (3) Realize your marriage is more important than your personal happiness. God did create marriage to offer fulfillment and personal pleasure, but He also intended the family to become living examples of Christ's relationship with His Church. Therefore, Marriage is God's institution for our good and His glory. If happiness is our primary goal, than we would get a divorce as soon as happiness goes out the window, so to speak. Marriage is for a life-time, <u>till death do us part</u>.

According to statistics today, the average length of time for a marriage is eight years and only four and a half percent of marriages reach the 50 year plateau or what is referred to as the Golden Anniversary. As a result of how the institution of marriage has deteriorated, more than two million people in the United States went through a divorce in 2016. The Bible has nothing good to say about divorce. We read in Malachi 2:16, *"For the Lord God of Israel says that He hates divorce, for it covers one's garment with violence," says the Lord of hosts, "Therefore take heed to your spirit, that you do not deal treacherously."*

Covenant

A Biblical marriage is a Holy Covenant, not a contract. A covenant is intended by God to be a lifelong fruitful relationship between a man and a woman. Marriage is a vow to God, to each other, our families and our community to remain steadfast in unconditional love, reconciliation and sexual purity, while faithfully growing in our covenant marriage relationship.

We can look and see there are many weddings taking place, but not many marriages. Some, however, have turned to God after a wedding has taken place and those couples have entered into a covenant with God later to form a real marriage. Most statistics show the divorce rate, as being in excess of 50% from the year 2010 till the present. If you are contemplating or considering marriage in the future, you should establish Biblical priorities and plan to receive sound Biblical counseling, as seen in <u>Proverbs 9:9</u>, *"Give instruction to a wise man, and he will be still wiser; teach a just man, and he will increase in learning."*

Even if you are presently in a marriage which is not on a high level, according to God's Word, you both should seek His will, so that marriage can thrive and prosper.

When we observe the courts and our higher judicial system today, we fail to see attorneys offering marriage or family counseling. They point directly toward focusing on divorce. This is where the Church needs to step up to the plate (so to speak) and preach, teach and offer wise counsel as mentioned in Proverbs 19:20, 21, *"Listen to counsel and receive instruction, that you may be wise in your latter days. There are many plans in a man's heart, Nevertheless the Lord's counsel --- **that will stand.**"*

<u>Note:</u> A simple way to better remember the word **Preach** is that 5/6 of Preach is **reach** and 4/6 is **each.** Thus, in preaching, we should strive to reach each with God's Word.

How Divorce Affects Children

We so often fail to realize the most important element of the family, when it experiences collapse and failure is that the children also suffer. Parents are to be examples and teachers according to the words found in Proverbs 22:6, *"Train up a child in the way he should go, And when he is old he will not depart from it."* **Divorce** is no small thing for children. What parents envision as a quick way out often results in emotional damage that the children will possibly carry throughout their entire lives.

Children have the attitude that their parents possess supernatural abilities. They tend to think no problem is too great for their parents to cope with. They believe there is only one right family relationship, and that is Dad and Mom being together. As a result of a divorce, most all children suffer in one way or another. Many suffer physical illness, others academically or both. Several engage in drugs or committing a crime as a juvenile. Some live in poverty. No matter how we may think, statistics don't lie when we speak of increased risks.

Second marriages, most times, brings on additional complications and raises the emotional levels of children, such as stepsiblings, stepparents, and step grandparents. Remember, in second marriages, the difficult adjustments are more difficult for children, because it is the adults who choose new mates and families, not the children. This is why parents should take a good long and extensive look before choosing divorce. What might appear to be like a simple solution to you could be a disaster for you and your children.

Can Any Hope Come from a Broken Family

If you or anyone has suffered from a divorce or a broken family, there is hope. We read in John 3:17, *"For God did not send His Son into the world to condemn the world, but that the world through Him might be saved."* This refers to the transforming power of the Holy Spirit.

If one or both have come from a broken home and are beginning together in marriage, any old script or resume from your past should be burned or destroyed. Instead, enter into your marriage with Biblical counseling, praying together, being passionate toward one another and allow for spontaneous responses. Learn to forgive, grow together and be a good teammate. Don't keep score, in other words, don't try to score brownie points; and when the other one makes mistakes, don't hold it against them. Cultivate interests together, by taking time to enjoy doing something your mate likes to do and vice versa. As the years pass, learn to celebrate the various milestones together and be sure to express your love to each other, each and every day. When your mate comes to you for advice concerning a problem, don't offer criticism, but rather offer a solution or ask God's guidance from His Word. Offer encouragement and practice complimenting each other. While it is good to spend quality time together and help your relationship grow stronger, it is also good to give each other space, so you will miss each other, as well as allowing each to grow in self-awareness.

***

> "God intends and expects marriage to be a lifetime commitment between a man and a woman, based on the principles of Biblical love. The relationship between Jesus Christ and His church is the supreme example of the committed love that a husband and wife are to follow in their relationship with each other."
>
> –John C. Broger

> "God created Marriage. No government subcommittee envisioned it. No social organi- zation developed it. Marriage was conceived and born in the mind of God."
>
> – Max Lucado

Guinness Book of World Records, Zelmyra and Herbert Fisher broke Guinness World Record for the longest marriage. They were married on May 13, 1924. In 2008 they earned the record at 84 years. In 2011, Herbert passed away at age 105 and two years later in 2013, Zelmyra followed at 105 years old as well. When Herbert passed, the couple had been married for 87 years. Prior to their death, they were interviewed about what it takes to have a beautiful marriage that lasts a lifetime and their answers were astoundingly simple______ **Question 1** What made you realize that you could spend the rest of your lives together? **Answer** "With each day that passed, our relationship was more solid and secure. Divorce was never an option, or even a thought." **Question 2** What was the best marriage advice you ever received? **Answer** "Respect, support and communicate with each other. Be faithful, honest and true. Love God and each other with all your heart." **Question 3** What is the fondest memory of your 85 year marriage? **Answer** "Our legacy: 5 children, 10 grandchildren, 9 great- grand children, and 1 great- great grandchild." **Question 4** What's the one thing you have in common that transcends everything else? **Answer** "We both are Christians and believe in God. Marriage is a commitment to the Lord. We pray with and for each other every day." **Conclusion:** Zelmyra and Herbert had an inspiring and loving marriage. After 87 years, it was clear that they were as in love as the day they were married.

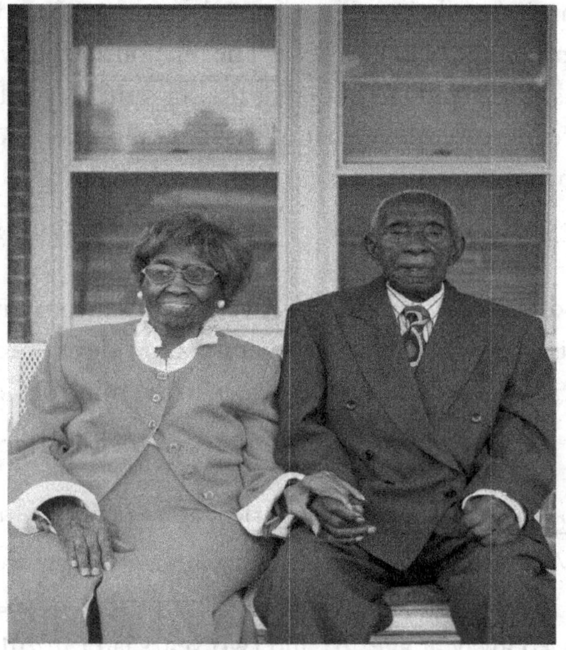

[Permission granted by Photographer, D.L. Anderson]

"A good marriage isn't something you find; it's something you make."

– **Gary L. Thomas**

Questions for Personal Evaluation or Group Discussion

Chapter 2

1. How would describe marriage?

2. Do the terms – Wedding Ceremony and Marriage mean the same thing?

3. Discuss the differences between a covenant and a contract.

Notes

CHAPTER III

"Childhood and Parenting"

"Train up a child in the way he should go, and when he is old he will not depart from it." (Proverbs 22:6)

Early Childhood

As newborn infants, there is suddenly that sweet look of innocence that fills the room. Then comes the short nights of sleep for the first-time parents, along with dirty diapers and sometimes, crying spells. However, what comes next is the fascinating and memorable opportunity to show that little tyke off and begin the all important educational process.

Between birth and three years of age the child typically doubles in height and quadruples in weight. During this time period the infant becomes a toddler with a more balanced, adult-like appearance. During these rapid physical changes, a typical three year old masters many skills, including walking, sitting, toilet training, using a spoon, hand-eye coordination to catch and throw a ball. This is also the time when they are able to begin learning about love, God's Word and songs of praise and worship.

Between three and five years of age, children grow very rapidly and begin to develop their motor skills. Motor skills may include the ability to skip and balance on one foot. Their physical growth tends to slow down between five and eight years of age, while their body and motor skills become more refined. This is also a time when they are more receptive to understanding God's Word and developing value systems. Also, between five and eight years of age, they can memorize large portions of Scripture, provided they are exposed to an atmosphere which is conducive to spiritual growth.

During the first three years, they develop a spoken vocabulary of between 300 and 800 words. By age five, a child's vocabulary increases to about 1200 to 1500 words and they can form sentences with five to seven words in them.

By age eight, some children, whose parents have spent quality time raising their children, and who have been around prayer and the Word of God, have developed a keen understanding of basic fundamentals of the Bible.

Language is a powerful tool to enhance cognitive development. Also, some parents use flash cards to help along those lines.

Middle Childhood (Eight to Twelve)

Most people believe this time stage in a child's life is a period in which their skills are further developed in perception of memory and inter-personal relationships. Deuteronomy 6:6-9, *"And these words which I command you today shall be in your heart. You shall teach them diligently to your children, and shall talk to them when you sit in your house, when you walk by the way, when you lie down, and when you rise up. You shall bind them as a sign on your hand, and they shall be as frontlets between your eyes. You shall write them on the doorposts of your house and on your gates."*

Physical development during middle childhood is less than in early childhood. Growth is slow until the onset of puberty. The onset of puberty differs across gender lines and begins earlier in females.

Middle childhood is a time when children develop competence in social relationships. They are strongly influenced by their parents and family in general, as they face peer pressure and learn how to adjust to the challenges of adolescence. They also begin to become more opinionated. This is the age when parents should have a marvelous opportunity to have open discussion regarding every subject matter, which concerns their child, especially the Way of Salvation and spiritual matters.

Adolescence (Twelve to Eighteen)

As individuals enter adolescence, they are confronted by diversified changes all at one time, it seems. They are undergoing physical growth, as well as cognitive growth. They are also facing new situations, responsibilities, and people. They begin to pull away from relying on their family, especially if their family is not grounded Biblically in the home and in a strong church family. This is when the family should offer a close source of identity with youth that are united with Jesus Christ, because wrong peer pressure can be devastating at this time in their life.

The impact of the media and social expectations on adolescent development is very strong today. Young people are bombarded with images of sex, violence, and measures of beauty which they find to be unattainable. Plus, public leaders, politicians, professional athletes and even so-called Christian pastors fail to be proper examples. Many times, without Godly parents, this type exposure leads adolescents to an increase in school violence, sexuality and eating disorders. Due to the strong ungodly influence within many public school systems today, several faith-based Christian parents are turning to home-schooling or that of private Christian schools.

Although, Christian education should begin at childbirth, it is essential to follow the guidelines in Deuteronomy 6:7, *"You shall teach them diligently to your children, and shall talk of them when you sit in your house, when you walk by the way, when you lie down, and when you rise up."* This passage emphasizes the ongoing nature of such instruction. It should be done at all times—at home, on the road, at night and in the morning. Biblical truth should be the foundation of our homes. By following the principles of these commands, we teach our children that worshiping God should be constant, not reserved for Sunday mornings or nightly prayers.

During the ages of twelve to eighteen, we often fail to realize how critical this time frame is to the lives within this age bracket. Many conflicts occur because of the emphasis which is placed on sports that have become like a god, along with our society allowing Sunday to become like any other day of the week.

While most people 65 years of age and younger have never heard of the **"Blue Law"** that was prevalent up until around the year 1960, many of those in their late sixties and older, have forgotten that the Blue Laws, also known as the Sunday laws, were designed to restrict or ban some or all Sunday activities for religious reasons. This was meant in particular to promote the observance of Sunday as being a day of worship or rest. Blue laws also restricted shopping or banned the sale of certain items on specific days, most on Sundays in the western world. Blue laws were enforced in parts of the United States and Canada, as well as some European countries, particularly in Austria, Germany, Switzerland, and Norway, keeping most stores closed on Sundays. Most blue laws have been repealed in the United States, although some states still ban the sale of alcoholic beverages or cars on Sundays.

As Christian parents, we have the influence to teach our children God's principles, so that God, the master potter, can form them as a piece of living clay. A young child's heart is tender and receptive to the instructions of a loving parent.

"Hand Molded"

Poem by Deborah Ann Belka

Hand Molded, each little curve made with love, so God we can serve. Formed out of clay, a vessel to be used ___in our hearts . . . God's Spirit was fused.

God is the potter, Christ is the mold and His ways . . .we're to keep and hold. Sometimes we crack, under the pressure ___but God will restore for we're His treasure.

Hand molded, grace's transformation__ renewed in His love by His sanctification.

<u>Isaiah 64:8</u> "But now, O Lord, You are our Father; we are the clay, and You our potter; and we are the work of Your hand."

Today, during this twenty-first century, there are sports activities and no limit to the various functions taking place on Sundays, which are to be set aside for worship to God and observed for a day of rest. Our children are suffering from such selfish thinking. God, who made us, is Holy. He is all knowing. *"For My people are foolish, they have not known me. They are silly children, and they have no understanding. They are wise to do evil, But to do good they have no knowledge" (Jeremiah 4:22).* "This idea of going to Harvard or some other prestigious university and getting the advice of some of the boys with high IQs is preposterous. Oh, we are wise in doing evil. God says that those who pretend to know Him and don't really know Him are foolish." __J. Vernon McGee, Through the Bible Commentary

Our children need to be taught the Word of God, while they are young. They should be taught to go to the house of God and not just to seek after the pleasures of this world, which are not eternal. The key word in the Book of Ecclesiastes is <u>Vanity</u>, which is the futile emptiness of trying to be happy apart from God.

The Bible tells us very clearly, *"For the message of the cross is foolishness to those who are perishing, but to us who are being saved it is the power of God. For it is written: 'I will destroy the wisdom of the wise, and bring to nothing the understanding of the prudent.' Where is the wise? Where is the scribe? Where is the disputer of this age? Has not God made foolish the wisdom of this world? For since, in the wisdom of God, the world through wisdom did not know God, it pleased God through the foolishness of the message preached to save those who believe."* (1 Corinthians 1:18-21).

Parenting

In essence, a parent is a caregiver of the offspring of their own species. It is the process of promoting and supporting the physical, emotional, social and intellectual development of a child from infancy to adulthood.

Even though parenting skills vary, it only seems reasonable that all parents should study and follow God's Word, the Bible, in order to develop good parenting skills. *"Correct your son and he will give you rest; yes, he will give delight to your soul."* (Proverbs 29:17)

God has made each one of our children special in his or her own unique way. Our role as parents isn't seeking to have them be perfect. Our main goal is to ensure our children are everything God intended them to be. So with this in mind, we should raise our children in a manner that will cultivate their hearts toward serving God. The Apostle Paul said to the early church to imitate him as he imitated Christ. Our children will most likely follow the path we have taken and perhaps will take the same road we are presently traveling. Providing we are following in the footsteps of Christ, our children will be so intrigued and cultivated that they will also. While there is no guarantee they will do so, it is up to us to follow the Scriptures and in doing such we may sow the seed in order to present them the opportunity of eternal life. A Father has a great effect upon his children! Notice the following illustration:

<u>*A Young Child Wanted to go to Church*</u>

There was a story once told me about a child who kept asking his parents to take him to church. He said, "they teach us there of Jesus' love, of how He died for all, upon the cruel cross to save those who on Him will call." "Not today", his dad replied, I've worked hard all week, and I must rest; and I'm going fishing, so I can relax. Don't bother me; we'll go to church some day." Several years passed and the small child grew up. His parents then decided it was time to go to church, but the child was no longer interested. Now that the parents are growing older and those young childhood days have passed, the parents miss hearing the excitement in the child's voice that used to ring out. Instead, they hear the same reply from him that once came from their mouths, "I'm too busy, perhaps I'll go someday."

The parents now brush the tears from their eyes, as they can still hear the plead from what was once a sweet little boy saying, "Please take me to church and Sunday School." It's too late and now those days can no longer be retrieved.

(Something to Ponder ON)

What the Bible Says About Good Parents

The Bible is very thorough and complete in detailing how parents are to successfully raise their children to become Godly men and women. **First**, a good parent is to teach them that the Word of God is true and necessary. **Second**, we need to be a godly example by committing ourselves to His commands and begin with the command of Deuteronomy 6:7-9 by teaching our children to do the same. **Third**, we are to teach our children the roles of husbands and wives, which are to be respectful of and submissive to each other as in (Ephesians 5:21). **Fourth**, God has stated there is *authority* to establishing and keeping order in the home. *"But I want you to know that the head of every man is Christ, the head of woman is man, and the head of Christ is God" (1Corinthians 11:3).* This passage is saying that Christ is not inferior to God and neither is the wife inferior to her husband. God is teaching that without submission to authority, there is no order. By being the head of the household the responsibility of the husband is to love his wife as he loves his own body, in the same way that Christ loved the church (Ephesians 5:25-29). In regards to this loving leadership, it shouldn't be difficult for the wife to submit to her husband's authority (Ephesians 5:24; Colossians 3:18). Her utmost responsibility is to love and respect her husband, while living in wisdom and purity, and take care of the home (Titus 2:4-5). Since women are naturally more nurturing than men because they were designed to be the primary caretakers of their children. **Fifth**, discipline and instruction are important parts of being a good parent. *"He who spares his rod hates his son, but he who loves him disciplines him promptly* (Proverbs 13:24). When children are raised in homes without discipline they tend to feel unloved and not valued. As they grow older they rebel and have little or no respect for authority, including God's. Proverbs 19:18 *says, "Chasten your son while there is hope, and do not set your heart on his destruction."* **Sixth**, while discipline is needed, it must be balanced with love or children will grow up resentful, and rebellious (Colossians 3:21). Discipline is painful when it is taking place (Hebrews 12:11), but if administered in love, it is very beneficial to the child. *"Fathers, do not provoke your children to wrath, but bring them up in the training and admonition of the Lord"* (Ephesians 6:4). **Seventh**, it is also very important to involve your children in a good Bible-believing church family while they are young, attending regularly (Hebrews 10:25). They need to see you studying the Word, as well as studying it with them. As parents, you should discuss the world around them, as they will see it from their perspective and have questions. You should also teach them about the glory of God through everyday life. They also need to follow your example in obeying and worshipping the Lord.

Some Final Summarization and Points to Remember

Children who experience love find it easier to believe God loves them. A child who is allowed to be disrespectful to his parents will not show true respect for anyone. No parent is perfect. We all can look back and recall things we could have done to help our children be better prepared for adulthood. It is best to admit it to them and encourage them to learn from our mistakes.

Children need love and love is not weak, sporadic or insincere; rather it is tender, passionate, strong, sincere and should be patterned after God's love, as recorded in 1 John 4:7-8 and John 3:16.

Some Suggestions: (1) Point your children to Christ as early as possible, by providing the atmosphere of a peaceful home and sharing the Christ of Calvary with them. (2) Play with them. (3) Establish wonderful memories, by taking time with them in their favorite family activities. Have game night, family devotions before bedtime, family pictures, showing interest in each other's desires, and form family rituals they will remember. (4) Discipline and correction enforces limits, which really teaches children how to behave in an unruly world. Discipline is not punishment. It helps them to become competent, caring and in control. (5) Have time with Dad – when they engage with fathers they do better in school, they learn to solve problems more successfully and generally cope better with whatever comes in life. (6) Help them to manage their time sufficiently. (7) Read books with them. Start when they are newborns and form a bond with them involving books, so to set them up for a lifetime of reading. (8) Always tell them the truth. (9) Teach them to say – "I Love You", "Thank You", "I'm Sorry", and teach them to communicate properly by writing notes and letters, as well as to acknowledge when others show kindness toward them. (10) Teach them to be Polite by saying – "Please", "Yes Sir, No Sir and Yes Ma'am, No Ma'am", "Excuse me", and teach them to hold a door open for older people. (11) To apologize when making a mistake. (12) You should kiss and hug your spouse in front of your children, as your marriage is the only example your child has of what a loving relationship looks and sounds like. Don't allow the television to be their example. (13) Establish from the beginning a strong and healthy church family relationship. (14) Give Praise occasionally, instead of just saying, "You're Great" – try and be specific about what your child did to receive a special compliment. (15) Sometimes it's O.K. to say "NO" to your extra obligations. You will never regret spending more time with your children. (16) Don't spoil your child. No child is the center of the Universe. (17) Teach your child to be a responsible citizen. (18) Values are important. Teach them to go out of their way to help others in need. (19) Love your children equally, but treat them uniquely, as they are individuals. (20) Our children are not ours; they are only lent to us for a time period. As parents, we are only here to help them grow up and mature. We are to remind them, all of us are placed on this earth to Glorify God.

Responsibilities of Good Parents

During these formative years is when parents have a great opportunity to instill strong values and Biblical fundamentals in their children. This is because in a child's early years, they want to please their parents, compared to their early school years when they try to fit in with their peers. Also, it is during these pre-school years the parents need to converse with their children, as adults rather than communicating to them as if they were still babies.

Many times from infancy to age five years, children are placed in front of a television or around the wrong type of music, which is not a conducive environment for teaching and learning for young children. Many stay-at-home moms provide a safe, responsive and nurturing environment to support the learning and development of their infant, toddler or preschooler. This is accomplished by teaching them children's Bible songs and reading Bible stories, along with taking time to dialogue for a short time, before quiet time.

Working parents should allow some quality time each evening with their child or children before putting them to bed, so as to offer a bonding and nurturing, which is important to their brain development, as well as their social, emotional and cognitive development. Pray with them, hug them and tuck them in bed.

As the children grow through the middle school and adolescence years into young adults, they need to know they have parents that they can confide in and always look up to out of honor and respect for being Godly parents. Parent-child relationships can be very rewarding, as well as very challenging at times. The Bible does offer some excellent guidelines in regards to parent-child relationships. Of course, we can know that God is the perfect Father who disciplines in love and has promised to always be with us.

> *"Each day of our lives we make deposits in the memory banks of our children."*
>
> – Chuck Swindoll

Teaching Good Work Ethics

Children tend to learn work ethics from their parents in a subconscious manner through various situations. Just as having parents with strong religious beliefs, as well as things such as good hygiene. A lot of rebellion comes about when parents are either too authoritarian, or too permissive. We teach our children best by being good examples along with dialogue with substance. Hard work habits do not always include physical labor, but rather working hard at what one is attempting to achieve through consistency. For example, the old analysis of the man who asked the question – "Which would you rather have, a million dollars or a penny and double it every day for 30 days?" The theory here is that a penny is practically nothing, however, patience and consistent growth for a period of time makes that penny very valuable. In reality, we start with nothing and work diligently and consistently to achieve our goal. Example, the penny doubled every day for the first ten days is only $5.12, on the twentieth day $5,242.88, by the twenty-seventh day $671,088.64, but on day thirty it becomes $5,368,709.12. Note: Even though this analogy is not practical in the truest sense, it expresses the need for our being vigilant in our work ethics. Have you ever heard the old saying, "You can't accomplish everything in a day, but you need to work every day at it?"

We must remember our values are not our own; they are passed down from generations, if we don't rebel and we maintain this consistency. In the book of Proverbs 10:4-5 we read, *"He who has a slack hand becomes poor, but the hand of the diligent makes rich. He who gathers in summer is a wise son; he who sleeps in harvest is a son who causes shame."*

Patience is a Virtue

There is an old saying, "Be the parent today that you want your children to remember tomorrow." Our children deserve our time, so we should keep this in mind as we seek to guide them each day and offer the instruction they need in order that they might cultivate their own garden of wisdom.

> "Good character is not formed in a week or a month. It is created little by little, day by day. Protracted and patient effort is needed…"
>
> – Heraclitus

"WE NEED TO INSTRUCT OUR DAUGHTERS TO RECOGNIZE THE DIFFERENCE BETWEEN"

A man who sweet-talks her and a man,
who commends her,

A man who solicits her
and a man who respects her,

A man who sees her as a possession,
and a man, who looks at her appropriately,

A man who only sexually desires her
and a man who really loves her,

A man who is struck on himself
and a man who values her
as a gift to him.

And then we need to instruct our sons
to be that kind of man.

Questions for Personal Evaluation or Group Discussion

Chapter 3

1. At what age can a child be taught the Bible and become a Christian?

2. How long does it take to mold a child into becoming a Christian?

Notes

CHAPTER

IV

"The Spiritual Aspect of Life"

"A man by his sin may waste himself, which is to waste that which on earth is most like God. This is man's greatest tragedy and God's heaviest grief."

– A. W. Tozer

From the minute we are born, we are dying and the very moment we are born again we are really beginning to live. We read in the Gospel of John 3:3-- *Jesus said…"Most assuredly, I say to you, unless one is born again, he cannot see the Kingdom of God."*

Just as there are physical laws that govern the physical universe, so are there spiritual laws that govern your relationship with God. In a moment we will uncover those spiritual laws, but first we need to know that two thousand years ago, our loving Creator, God, kept His promise of Genesis 3:15 as He stepped into history in the person of His Son, Jesus Christ: *"In the beginning was the Word, and the Word was with God, and the Word was God…And the Word became flesh and dwelt among us, and we beheld His glory, the glory as of the only begotten of the Father, full of grace and truth" (John 1:1, 14).*

God wrapped himself in the flesh of His creation to become the sinless sacrifice to die for the sins of the world.

"For God so loved the world that He gave His only begotten Son, that whosoever believes in Him should not perish but have everlasting life" (John 3:16).

Law #1 – God **Loves** you and offers a wonderful **plan** for your life. Christ said, *"I have come that they may have life, and that they may have it more abundantly" (John 10:10).*

Law #2 – Man is **sinful** and **separated** from God. Therefore, he cannot know and experience God's love and plan for his life. *"All have sinned and fall short of the glory of God" (Romans 3:23).* Man was created to have fellowship with God; but, because of his own stubborn self-will, he chose to go his own independent way and fellowship with God was broken. Man became separated, *"The wages of sin is death" (Romans 6:23).*

Law #3 – Jesus Christ is God's **only** provision for man's sin. Through Him you can know and experience God's love and plan for your life. He died in our place. *"God demonstrates His own love toward us, in that while we were still sinners, Christ died for us" (Romans 5:8). "Christ died for our sins...He was buried...He was raised on the third day, according to the Scriptures...He appeared to Peter, then to the twelve. After that He appeared to more than five hundred..." (1 Corinthians 15:3-6. Jesus said, "I am the way, and the truth, and the life; no one comes to the Father but through Me" (John 14:6).*

Law #4 – We must individually **receive** Jesus Christ as Savior and Lord; then we can know and experience God's love and plan for our lives. *"As many as received Him, to them He gave the right to become children of God, even to those who believe in His name" (John 1:12).* We receive Christ through Faith. *"By grace you have been saved through faith; and that not of yourselves, it is the gift of God; not as a result of works that no one should boast" (Ephesians 2:8, 9).*

Jesus' life was everything the prophets foretold. The sinless Son of God was born of the Virgin Mary, grew in knowledge and stature, and began His public ministry when He was in His thirties. During His ministry, Jesus healed the sick, restored the blind, raised the dead, and told them how they could receive eternal life. He did these miraculous acts to show that He truly was the Son of God.

"And truly Jesus did many other signs in the presence of His disciples, which are not written in this book; but these are written that you may believe that Jesus is the Christ, the Son of God, and that believing you may have life in His name" (John 20:30, 31).

The time came for Jesus to become the perfect sacrifice – to die for the sins of the world and to restore that broken relationship between God and man. He willingly paid the penalty that we would have had to pray for our sin (Romans 6:23).

While nailed on the cross, just before He died, Jesus cried, *"It is finished!"* (*Tetelestai*) (John 19:30). This Greek work means, "paid in full".

But it didn't end there on the cross. Jesus was buried in the tomb, but after three days He rose from the dead, conquering death. *"He is not here; for He is raised" (Matthew 28:6).* Prior to this, a person had to offer a temporary sacrifice of unblemished animals, but no longer was this necessary. The "Lamb of God", Jesus Christ, became the perfect and final sacrifice. You see, the Bible goes on to say, *"For since by man came death, by Man also came the resurrection of the dead. For as in Adam all die, even so in Christ all shall be made alive" (1 Corinthians 15:21-22).*

God offers us the opportunity to be forgiven, spotless and loved. When we understand and accept God's gift through His Son Jesus Christ, we have a restored relationship with God, our Creator. The Bible makes it clear: God's gift of Salvation is offered to us, not just to hear or agree with intellectually, but to respond to in faith (John 14:6; Romans 6:23). This gift is what we receive by faith (Ephesians 2:8-9; Titus 3:5).

For we all have sinned and God calls upon men everywhere to repent of their sin and place their faith in Christ. If we repent and believe we will have our sins forgiven. The Bible makes clear the eternal destiny of those who reject Him. They will be separated from Him forever in a place called Hell (Revelation 20:15).

What is Religion?

This is a term that is misused, abused, and quite ambiguous at times. For instance, back in the Old Testament days and during Christ's time on earth, there were those who practiced being religious in the synagogues, as well as those in the churches, temples, cathedrals and various meeting halls in today's world.

Religion can be defined in the following manner --- There is no scholarly consensus over what precisely constitutes a **religion**. It may be defined as cultural system of designated behaviors and practices, world views, texts, sanctified places, prophesies, ethics, or organizations, that relate humanity to the supernatural, transcendental, or spiritual. Religious practices may include rituals, sermons, commemoration or veneration (of deities), sacrifices, festivals, feasts, trances, initiations, funeral services, matrimonial services, meditation, prayer, music, art, dance, public service, or other aspects of human culture. Traditionally, faith, in addition to reason, has been considered a source of religious beliefs. There are an estimated 10,000 distinct religions worldwide, but about 84% of the world's population is affiliated with one of the six largest religions, namely Christianity, Catholicism, Judaism, Islam, Hinduism, Buddhism, or forms of folk religion. Shinto is a religion that is unique to Japan. Pantheism, Atheism and many other cults are sometimes referred to in a religious manner.

Note: Even many religious orders are thought as being Christian, while they are in no way even close to following the Scriptural text of the Bible. We might be correct in saying the term – Religion, is so diversified that it is deceptive and goes without comment that Jesus Christ was sent into the world to do away with religion.

> *"Religion today is not transforming people; rather it is being transformed by the people. It is not raising the moral level of society, it is descending to society's own level, and congratulating itself that it has scored a victory because society is smilingly accepting its surrender."*
>
> **– A. W. Tozer**

What is a Christian?

As Christians we believe the Bible is the inerrant, infallible inspired Word of God. The disciples were first called Christians in Antioch, according to Acts 11:26, *"...And the disciples were first called Christians in Antioch."* This was because they were willing to suffer and lay down their lives for Jesus Christ, the Son of God.

As Jesus taught: *"And this is eternal life, that they may know You, the only true God, and Jesus Christ whom You have sent" (John 17:3).* Read John *Chapter 17* in its entirety. This passage is where Jesus prays for Himself, then for His disciples and last for All Believers. Here, Jesus is praying to God, His Father, as they are part of the trinity.

Our Spiritual Aspect

Our spiritual aspect is our inner essence, our soul, the part of us that is eternal. The unmistakable teaching of the Bible is that all people, whether they are saved or lost, will exist eternally, in either heaven or hell. *"For if the dead do not rise, then Christ is not risen and if Christ is not risen, your faith is futile (or in vain); you are still in your sins! Then also those who have fallen asleep in Christ have perished. If in this life only we have hope in Christ, we are of all men the most pitiable" (1 Corinthians 15:16-19).* **Note:** While all souls are immortal, it is important to remember that we are not eternal in the same way that God is. God is the only truly eternal being in that He alone is without a beginning or end. Jesus tells us in Matthew 10:28, *"And do not fear those who kill the body but cannot kill the soul. But rather fear Him who is able to destroy both soul and body in hell."*

It is very interesting to note what John, on the isle of Patmos, saw in Revelations 20:4, *"... Then I saw the souls of those who had been beheaded for their witness to Jesus and for the Word of God, who had not worshiped the beast or his image, and had not received his mark on their foreheads or on their hands. And they lived and reigned with Christ for a thousand years."* And the Apostle Paul mentions in Romans 6:23, *"For the wages of sin is death, but the gift of God is eternal life in Christ Jesus our Lord."*

Spiritual Growth

In order for spiritual growth to occur, you first need to possess a true spiritual life in having faith in the Lord Jesus Christ. *"And this is the testimony: that God has given us eternal life, and this life is in His Son. He who has the Son has life; he who does not have the Son of God does not have life" (1 John 5:11-12).*

Then to continue to grow you should increase in your knowledge and understanding of God's Word. Seek God's Will, which is to become more like Him. We can better grow with the details provided in 2 Peter 1:3-8, *"His divine power has given to us all things that pertain to life and godliness, through the knowledge of Him who called us by glory and virtue, by which have been given to us exceedingly great and precious promises, that through these you may be partakers of the divine nature, having escaped the corruption that is in the world through lust. But also for this very reason, giving all diligence, add to your faith virtue, to virtue knowledge, to knowledge self-control, to self-control perseverance, to perseverance godliness, to godliness brotherly kindness, and to brotherly kindness love. For if these things are yours and abound, you will be neither barren nor unfruitful in the knowledge of our Lord Jesus Christ."*

When we neglect and refuse to grow in our spiritual life, we tend to manufacture our own problems that eventually destroy what God has created – "Life". In other words, if we fail to plan, we plan to fail. There are no options.

Spiritual Discipline

Jesus said to Thomas, *"I am the way, the truth, and the life" (John 14:6).* It is only practical that we submit to spiritual discipline, just as an athlete does to physical training. When Christ said, "Follow Me", He meant it. It only makes sense to do what He did, since Jesus taught that our spiritual life takes place in our physical life as well as in our heart. A disciplined life does not in any way earn us favor with God or measure spiritual success. Just like physical exercises, spiritual exercises equip us to live fully and freely in our everyday reality of God. There can be no spiritual discipline without first submitting to the Holy Spirit. We should set aside time where we can grow spiritually through prayer, Bible study, and a place of solitude. This contemporary culture we live in today is anything but free from a maze of noise and the constant use of technological devices. We need to become a member of the **3-C club**...Calm, Cool and Collective.

As an example of my military discipline, as well as family training, the following illustration offers a good example for the proper understanding of **NO** and **YES: No** is used to express denial or refusal. So to clear it up in a more precise manner when the word **No** is used, we should perhaps ask the question... "What is it about **NO** you fail to understand, is it the **N** or the **O**? Answer: The **N** stands for Non-negotiable and the **O** stands for omit. Non-negotiable is defined as not open for discussion. **Yes** is an affirmative answer or to give approval. A synonym is absolutely. We could offer a further breakdown for **YES** with: **Y** stands for You. **E** stands for Excitedly. **S** stands for Should. Yes, **You Excitedly Should.**

Note: The above mentioned advice should be understood as coming from those having Christ-like authority, such as Christian parents, who are being disciplined by the Word of God. It is beneficial to be obedient and submissive to those who have rule over you in the Lord, especially parents. This is the first commandment with promise ____ *"Honor your father and your mother, that your days may be long upon the land which the Lord your God is giving you" (Exodus 20:12)* and *"Honor your father and mother, which is the first commandment with promise: that it may be well with you and you may live long on the earth" (Ephesians 6:2).*

> *"Gradual growth in grace, growth in knowledge, growth in faith, growth in love, growth in holiness, growth in humility, growth in spiritual-minded, all this I see clearly taught and urged in Scripture, and clearly exemplified in the lives of*

many of God's saints. But sudden, instantaneous leaps from conversion to consecration I fail to see in the Bible."

–J.C. Ryle

"Instead of dwelling on the things you didn't get after praying, think of the countless blessings God has given you without you even asking."

"The ways, and fashions, and amusements of the world have a continually decreasing place in the heart of a growing Christian. He does not condemn them as downright sinful, nor say those who have anything to do with them are going to hell. He only feels they have a constantly diminishing hold on his own affections and gradually seem smaller and more trifling in his eyes."

–J.C. Ryle

"If I had a choice, I would still choose to remain blind...for when I die, the first face I will ever see will be the face of my blessed Savior. It seemed intended by the Providence of God that I should be blind all my life, and I thank Him for the dispensation."

– Fanny Crosby

Questions for Personal Evaluation or Group Discussion

Chapter 4

1. Can the terms Religion and Christianity become confusing? How?

2. What is meant by Spiritual Discipline in the contemporary culture we live in today?

Notes

CHAPTER

V

"The Physical Aspect of Life"

"I will praise You, for I am fearfully and wonderfully made; Marvelous are Your works, and my soul knows well my frame was not hidden from You..." (Psalms 139:14-15).

Although there are many topics and studies about the human body, we will be observing two different viewpoints in this chapter, namely, the maintenance and the ownership of such. By maintenance, we should (if possible) take care of our bodies, especially since we read in 1 Corinthians 6:19, *"...Do you not know that your body is the temple of the Holy Spirit who is in you, whom you have from God, and you are not your own?"* By ownership, we must realize as a child of God that our body belongs to Him.

Our Body, the Temple of the Holy Spirit

The apostle Paul exhorted the Christians in Corinth to flee from sexual immorality. The moment we place our trust and faith in Jesus Christ as our Savior, the indwelling of God's Spirit takes place (1 Corinthians 12:13). Our salvation is then sealed and guaranteed (Ephesians 1:13-14). The Holy Spirit will be with us forever (John 14:16), given by God as His pledge of the believer's future inheritance in glory

(2 Corinthians 1:21-22). By using the word "temple" instead of house or residence, Paul conveyed the idea that our bodies are a sacred place, in which the Spirit not only lives, but is worshiped, revered and honored. It also becomes very important how we behave, think and speak, and what we allow in the temple through our eyes and ears, since every thought, word and deed is in His view. Even though He will never leave us, it is possible to grieve the Holy Spirit (Ephesians 4:30). Also in verse 31-32, Paul instructed the Ephesians not to grieve the Holy Spirit by getting rid of all bitterness, rage and anger, brawling and slander, along with every form of malice.

While we may be athletes, office workers, factory workers, and teachers or employed in any other type work, we should (as Christians) take care of our physical bodies, both in a physical, as well as a spiritual manner.

Maintaining Our Physical Body

God created man with a physical body, which is an amazing human machine, residing in an amazing world. The human brain is the most complex *(if I may say, computer)* matter in the entire universe. The body has a framework of bone and cartilage, which is known as the skeleton. Our body even lubricates itself by manufacturing a jelly-like substance. In fact, this very moment we are having blood being pumped through hundreds of blood vessels (maybe thousands) from an organ called the heart. These blood vessels transport food and oxygen to all parts of the body. Yes, this body is a wonderful machine. How can anyone deny there is a God? Just think, only God, could design and.... *"Create man in His own image, in the image of God created He him, male and female created He them"* (Genesis 1:27). All this from raw materials can be found in "the dust of the ground." Man is God's masterpiece – the crown of His creation.

When we fail to eat properly and exercise our bodies in a moderate manner, we manufacture our own problems, in that we neglect to maintain what God has given us as a vehicle to carry His gospel, and avoid unnecessary fatigue and health problems. Let us consider the various foods we eat. The majority of today's society tends to live in 'hurry-up' mode rather than a more relaxed style of life. Therefore, they get caught up in the "fast food" game, instead of eating a balanced meal. It is so easy to enjoy the latter, by studying and observing what foods are healthy and knowing how to prepare them in a healthier fashion. Fast food establishments cook in grease and oils that are bad for our systems and that have been used over and over throughout the day. Many of these foods have high volumes of salt, sugar, and fat that drive our bad Cholesterol up. Many people are not aware that sugar, white flour and hydrogenated oils are three things that feed cancer cells. Every single human person on planet earth has cancer cells in their bodies. The good news is that our body's natural defenses know how to defeat these tumor-causing cells, prior to their getting a chance to grow into a full-blown cancer.

Eating more fresh fruits and vegetables are helpful. Drinking plenty of water (preferably lemon water) is a great way to keep our kidneys flushed. Processed meats are not healthy.

Our bodies require that we get proper rest. We should also think on things that are good, since we read in Philippians 4:8 *"Finally, brethren, whatever things are true, whatever things are noble, whatever things are just, whatever things are pure, whatever things are lovely, whatever things are of good report, if there be any virtue and if there is anything praiseworthy, meditate on these things."* Thinking on good things allows our mind to dwell in peace. When our mind is dwelling on unclean things and we worry or fret, instead of placing our trust in God, our nerves can be affected, which affects our health in a negative manner.

Our bodies need exercise. There's an old saying, "If you don't use it, you'll lose it." Our bodies were made to work, not to sit on a couch. In our modern culture, many think they must go to a gym and pay out large sums of money in order to stay physically fit, while others simply walk at a fast gate and lift bricks or do exercises without costly equipment. Due to this technological age, many have jobs that require a lot of sitting at the desk, along with a longer work week and people do not move as much as they should, causing leg muscles to become immobile. When our circulation slows we burn fewer calories, thus those fat burners plummet. God made our legs to move. Literally, by way of obesity, heart disease, and diabetes, we are killing ourselves or at least minimizing our potential. If we are not careful, our posture becomes poor from not standing or walking properly. When you sit all day your hamstrings shorten and tighten causing your spine to become weak and stiff. It is no wonder, people in their late fifties and early sixties become less mobile and seem to give up on hiking, riding bicycles, and enjoying the things they once did. There are many people who have maintained their health and are still very active in their nineties. Any age past seventy is considered a bonus and we should constantly seek to glorify God, as we stay spiritually and physically fit. *"For bodily exercise profits a little, but godliness is profitable for all things, having promise of the life that now is and of that which is to come"(1 Timothy 4:8).*

Note: If while you are reading this chapter and feel that your time is not sufficient to fulfill this agenda, please reference Chapter 10 – "Time".

Staying active offers a better solution for keeping your metabolism moving the way God intended it to be. On the other hand, God is not concerned with our physical appearance or our health in the way our society is. 1 Samuel 16:7 says, *"...For the Lord does not see as man sees; for man looks at the outward appearance, but the Lord looks at the heart."* God is more concerned with our spiritual well-being, as Paul stated in First Timothy 4:6.

Years ago, people pondered two questions, (1) Are you so heavenly minded that you are no earthly good? and (2) Are you so earthly minded that you are no heavenly good? If so, then your life is out of balance. While all truth is God's truth, wherever it is found, the Scripture is the final authority. How do you define a healthy individual? What does the Bible say about it? Luke 2:52 says, *"And Jesus increased in wisdom and stature, and in favor with God and men."*

The Human Body's Five Senses

Most everyone has heard of and is familiar with the five senses of the human body: Sight, Sound, Smell, Taste and Touch. They seem to work independently, as distinct ways of perceiving the world. When one sense drops out, another can pick up the slack. For an example, people who are blind can train their hearing to perform double duty. Let's look at these senses individually_____ **Sight** – When our eyes are open, they take pictures of the world and send them to the brain to figure out what we are seeing. These images help us to understand the things around us, such as where to walk, colors, distances, the distinctions of people. **Sound** – We use our sense of hearing when we listen to music, talk with a friend, or hear the wind blowing. Different vibrations are passed to our brain where it processes the information so as we can determine or distinguish what sounds we hear. **Smell** -- Our nose is the organ that we use to smell. Smelling is also an aide in assisting us to taste. **Taste** – Our sense of taste comes from the taste buds on our tongue. Our tongue allows us to taste separate flavors: salty, sweet, sour and bitter. The tongue can identify textures and temperatures in our food like creamy, crunchy, hot or dry. Our tongue is also one of the strongest muscles in our body. It is able to heal from injury quicker than other parts of the body. The tongue also produces certain sounds when we speak or play certain instruments, such as the trumpet, clarinet or sax. **Touch** – The sense of touch is spread through the whole body. Nerve endings in the skin and in other parts of the body send information to the brain. There are four kinds of touch sensations that can be identified: cold, heat, contact and pain. Hair on the skin increase the sensitivity and can act as an early warning system for the body. People who are blind can use their sense of touch to read Braille. It's no wonder David said to God, *"I will praise You, for I am fearfully and wonderfully made, marvelous are Your works, and that my soul knows very well" (Psalms 139:14).*

There are Other Senses

Now that we have taken a look at the five most well known senses of the human body, let's take time to examine four others. One is sometimes referred to as the "sixth sense", which is called **Proprioception**. This sense is very important as it lets us know exactly where our body parts are and how to plan our movements. Such as being able to clap our hands together with our eyes closed or write with a pencil applying the correct pressure, and navigate through a narrow space. Another is known as the **Vestibular system**. This one explains the perception of our body in relation to gravity, movement and balance. This system measures acceleration, body movements and the head position. For example, it allows you to know you are in an elevator, or knowing whether you are lying down or sitting up.

The last two senses that are often mentioned, but rarely understood are: **Non-Sense** and **Common-Sense.**

Non-sense, which is defined as words or language having no meaning or conveying no intelligible ideas, conduct that is senseless, foolish, or absurd. Non-sense is no sense. Someone said, "Usually, when the plain sense makes perfect sense, seek no other sense, for the rest is non-sense."

What is **Common-sense** and does anyone possess it? It is defined as the ability to behave in a sensible way and make practical decisions. (Reference – Longman Dictionary)

(Verb Usage) – (1) Some people are brilliant thinkers, but they have no common-sense. (2) People don't always do what common-sense suggests. (3) Common-sense tells us that we should get more sleep. (4) Common-sense is what we think others possess. In other words, Common-sense is not so common.

* * *

"Nonsense is so good only because common sense is so limited."

– Santayana Quotes

Questions for Personal Evaluation
or Group Discussion

Chapter 5

1. From a Christian standpoint, is our body really ours to do with as we please?

2. What does the Bible say about physical fitness?

3. Should we examine how our society views physical fitness?

4. In what ways do we take our God given senses for granted?

Notes

CHAPTER

VI

"Biblical Counseling/ Psychology"

"The anointing of the Holy Spirit is given to illuminate His Word, to open the Scriptures, and to place the spiritual man in direct communication with the mind of God."

– Charles Fox Parham

Isaiah 55:8, 9, *"For My thoughts are not your thoughts, nor are your ways My ways," says the Lord. "For as the heavens are higher than the earth, so are My ways higher than your ways, and My thoughts than your thoughts."*

There are as many neurons (nerve cells) in the brain as there are stars in the Milky Way galaxy. Of all the objects in the universe, the human brain is the most complex.

The Bible explains that God's supreme creation of man in Zechariah 12:1 is an example of His creative powers and His sovereign authority over His creation – "...Thus says the Lord, who stretches out the heavens, lays the foundation of the earth, and forms the spirit of man within him."

The spirit of man is unique. No animal has it. This is what makes us separate or different from the animal kingdom. We also have within us a spirit that wants to know our Creator. God tells us to seek Him and He says we are to be found in Him. Acts 17:26-29, *"From one man He (God) made every nation of man to dwell on all the face of the earth, and has determined their pre-appointed times and the boundaries of their dwellings, so that they should seek the Lord, in the hope that they might grope for Him and find Him, though He is not far from each one of us; for in Him we live and move and have our being, as also some of your own poets have said, 'For we are also His offspring'. Therefore, since we are the offspring of God, we ought not to think that the Divine Nature is like gold or silver or stone, something shaped by art and man's devising."*

> How could anyone doubt the validity of God, in that only He could create this extremely complex structure, known as the human brain? "The human brain is a 3-pound mass of jelly-like fats and tissues. Up to one trillion nerve cells work together and coordinate the physical actions and mental processes that set humans apart from the species."
>
> – **National Geographic**

Paul and Psychology

"Let this same mind be in you which was also in Christ Jesus" (Philippians 2:5).

The study of psychology deals with the mind, its senses and human behavior. Since our mind controls our behavior and our behavior influences and is influenced in many ways, it becomes very interesting to examine the life of the Apostle Paul. As we watch news on television and read the newspapers, we somewhat understand what is going on in the world, concerning the problems that youth of today experience, the drugs, and all that goes with it. But, as Christians, we are still human beings and we are sometimes caught up with the very same problems that the world faces.

The Bible is not a textbook on psychology; rather it is about God and His relationship to mankind, whom He has created. Much is mentioned in the Bible about human behavior, and the Bible speaks with final authority.

Our Emotions

We all live in a world which is filled with fears and problems, but God our Creator, has an answer for all these problems. There are four types of emotions common to all, especially if we do not follow the principles of God's Word. If we reject God's guidelines, these emotions will destroy us. Let's consider these: (1) Such as the fear/anxiety syndrome, in which the world to a great degree, thinks all individuals are only a number and there is no help for mankind. Therefore, because we think like this, we have fears and anxiety attacks, as to what we may face. (2) The next group of emotions is the anger/hostility syndrome, since we are afraid. As a result, we tend to display our fears through anger, hostility and hatred. (3) Many suffer from a depression/guilt syndrome and as a result many people are in hospital beds, not because of physical illness, but rather that of emotional problems. For the non-believer or non-Christian, it could be a sense of guilt, that person may not recognize or acknowledge. As for the Christian, depression and guilt feelings may result from unconfessed sin in his or her life. (4) An emotional form of egotism (desiring to build up one's self-ego) is often used in order to combat fear.

When examining these four types of emotions and how to overcome them, we should first look at how to apply God's Word, since He made us. In doing so, let's focus on these four emotions seriatim. (1) The first emotional need that we have to be fulfilled is that of **affection**. We need to love and to be loved. Every baby born into this world needs and desires this. This is why God gave to us mothers, to breast-feed babies, not only for the benefit of the mother's milk that the baby receives, but for that sense of security the baby enjoys, as it is embraced in the mother's arms. That is something no bottle will ever accomplish, and every human being needs affection not only as babies. Isaiah 49:15, *"Can a woman forget her nursing child, and not have compassion on the son of her womb? Surely they may forget, yet I will not forget you."* (2) The second emotion that needs to be fulfilled is that of **acceptance,** of which one is, and each individual's character. Ephesians 2:19, *"Now, therefore, you are no longer strangers and foreigners, but fellow citizens with the saints and members of the household of God."* (3) Thirdly, we need to be **appreciated.** Luke 12:7, *"But the very hairs of your head are all numbered. Do not fear; you are of more value than many sparrows."* (4) We all need **achievement**, not only a sense of satisfaction or accomplishment, but also that which is praiseworthy. Philippians 1:6, *"Being confident of this very thing, that He who has begun a good work in you will complete it until the day of Jesus Christ."*

Note: There are three main reasons for which the Bible was written. First, God gave it to show the entrance and problem of Sin; Second, to show mankind the need for and the provision of Salvation; and Third, to provide for the Christian the right way to Sanctification of life. The *Greek* word for "Sanctify" is the same word translated "Holy". And the words "Holy" and "Sanctify" are synonymous terms in Scripture, which mean, 'to be set apart from evil and to be set apart unto God'.

The Bible verses Psychology

When we look at the Word of God three messages are presented in this order: **Sin** – first, we need to know that we all are sinners, who needs a Savior. **Salvation** - God has provided Salvation through the Lord Jesus Christ for our sins and once a person becomes a child of God, it is anticipated that he or she will lead a **Sanctified** life. This is why Christ stated in John 10:10, *"...I have come that they may have life, and that they may have it more abundantly."*

Each problem raised by life has its answer in the Word of God.

The book of Philippians provides the answers to overcoming the four emotions mentioned earlier that plague people and fulfill the emotions that one needs. (1) Chapter 1, verse 21, deals with Personal Identification, which has to do with **affection**____*"For to me, to live is Christ, and to die is gain."* Paul was identified with the Lord Jesus Christ in every aspect of his life. He was affected by what Christ had done for him; it affected his whole life. It changed him from being an employee of the Roman government, on the Damascus road committing people to prison under the name of Saul, and it transformed him so that now he was the Apostle Paul, preaching the Gospel of Christ. (2) Chapter 2, verse 5, answers the second emotional need, which is **acceptance** ___ *"Let this mind be in you which was also in Christ Jesus."* Here, Paul is saying, he had been accepted by Almighty God, as a child of God and an heir to His throne. (3) The third emotion that needs to be satisfied is that of **appreciation.** This is considered in Philippians Chapter 3, verses 13, 14, which answer the problem of Personal Priorities in life. While we all live in a very busy world today and seem to be caught up in multiple involvements, as well as choices in relation to our priorities, it tends to cause frustration in our lives. This frustration leads to depression, anxieties and fears, which may result in guilt feelings, and there are many negative reactions from which there is seemingly no escape. Here is where Paul says, *"Brethren, I do not count myself to have apprehended; but this one thing I do, forgetting those things which are behind and reaching forward to those things which are ahead, I press toward the goal for the prize of the upward call of God in Christ Jesus."* Then in verse 20, he says, *"For our citizenship is in heaven, from which we also eagerly wait for the Savior, the Lord Jesus Christ."* (4) In Chapter 4, Paul answers the fourth emotional need that every individual seems to have and that is **achievement.** It also offers personal security. Achievement gives to a person a certain sense of security. In Philippians 4:13, he states, *"I can do all things through Christ who strengthens me."* Paul did not mean by this he could do anything. No, all people have limitations, but all have certain talents, gifts and abilities. God does not measure these abilities. Every individual has certain responsibilities before God, and God has given every individual the talents and abilities to carry out the responsibilities that He has entrusted to us. It makes no difference whether one is the president or the janitor of a factory. Wherever God has placed us that is our responsibility. In Philippians 2:12, 13, the Apostle Paul admonishes us to, *"...work out your own salvation with fear and trembling; for it is God who works in you both to will and to do for His own good pleasure."* God both shows us His will through His Spirit and at the same time enables us to carry out His will through the talents that He has entrusted to us.

There are four things that provide God's children the standard for the Christian life: (1) for us to live worthy of the gospel, (2) that we stand fast in the faith, (3) that we are not terrified by what is coming, and (4) that we are willing to suffer for the Lord Jesus Christ. As Paul says in Philippians 1:21, *"For to me, to live is Christ, and to die is gain."*

The Church and Psychology

First, let's define each. The word **Church** (in the Christian sense) in the noun form, feminine gender – *ekklesia*, means in a short definition, 'a called out body, belonging to the Lord God'. The Church is not a building, but a body of believers with a specific nature and purpose. This body has biblical roles that are foundational in worship, edification and evangelism.

Worship is God-centered and Christ-centered, which is to praise and glorify God in worship, such as referenced in Hebrews 10:25, *"Not forsaking the assembling of ourselves together, as the manner of some, but exhorting one another, and so much the more as you see the Day approaching."*

Edification is a role of the church that involves nurturing, building up and helping believers to mature in Christ. Our churches are to do this through offering a variety of ministries such as Bible study, intercessory prayer, acts of genuine hospitality and more.

Evangelism means reaching to a lost world with compassion, sharing the Good News about Jesus Christ. Since people have questions or doubts about Christ, evangelism is "fishing for men" or "reaching the lost at any cost". This is a way to help them know the Truth, because Jesus is the Way, the Truth and the Life and by spreading the gospel of Christ, we are providing a method to feed and supply nourishment to the hungry souls of mankind.

A healthy church honors God and His intentions for His Church by implementing these three roles just mentioned.

When we look at the greatest commandment in Deuteronomy 6:5, *"You shall love the Lord your God with all your heart, with all your soul, and with all your strength"*, perhaps we should think that failing to love God with one's entire heart, soul, and might must be the greatest **sin** of which one could be guilty. In essence, not loving God is the root of all sin or evil. In summation of the Ten Commandments there should not be a condemnation only for atheists and pagans, but also for most Christians, as well, especially since we give such little love to God.

Jesus said, the second commandment is like to the first: *"You shall love your neighbor as yourself" (Matthew 22:39).* This command is essentially the evidence of truly loving God. John reminds us in 1 John 4:20, *"If someone says, 'I love God,' and hates his brother, he is a liar; for he who does not love his brother whom he has seen, how can he love God whom he has not seen?"* Loving your neighbor is the result of loving God. Jesus said in Matthew 22:40, *"On these two commandments hang all the Law and the Prophets."* Were it not for God's grace and the redemptive work of Christ, this teaching from Scripture would hang over us like a death sentence. We have disobeyed these two commandments and the penalty for sin is death, which is eternal separation from God and from the life and love which is in Him alone. Oh, how much we need a Savior.

Today's churches are constantly conducting conferences and workshops where various subjects from prosperity to prophecy, from miracles to marriage counseling and from healing to holiness are being taught and discussed. However, the subject of loving God seems to be absent. Instead, there appears to be a great deal of emphasis upon loving self – which was unheard of in the church until these last few years where Christian Psychology came into play.

Jesus said, *"On these two commandments*____ (1) first, loving God; (2) loving neighbor____ *hang all the law and the prophets" (Matthew 22:40).* Nothing more needed to be added. Yet there has been a third added – the love of self. About forty or fifty years ago, a man named Erich Fromm, a anti-Christian humanistic psychologist, who began teaching we must first love ourselves before we can love others. To the contrary, Jesus was saying, give your neighbors some of the attention you are giving yourselves. But Fromm's perverted interpretation, through Christian psychology, gained a very subtle entrance into the church. Most everything that is taught in Psychology is diametrically opposed to the Word of God.

Secondly, we need to define the term, **Psychology.** It is the scientific study of the human mind and its functions, especially those affecting behavior in a given context.

Many pastors today are incorporating so-called Christian Psychology in the church, either by recommendation or providing office space within the church premises.

Psalm1:1 reads *"Blessed is the man who walks not in the counsel of the ungodly, nor stands in the path of sinners, nor sits in the seat of the scornful."* Let's break this verse down by making reference to the Commentary, "Through the Bible" with J. Vernon McGee… Blessed is the man or Happy is the man. Who walks not in the counsel of the ungodly – We are to walk by faith. Who are the ungodly? They are people who leave God out of their lives and have no fear or respect of God. They never turn to God in prayer; never thank Him for the food they eat or for life or health. Stands in the path of sinners. Sin means to "miss the mark." They don't quite live the way they should. They are the ones the Scripture speaks of when it says, *"There is a way which seems right to a man, but its end is the way of death" (Proverbs 14:12).* Again the Scriptures say, *"All the ways of man are clean in his own eyes…" (Proverbs 16:2).* Next, he sits in the seat of the scornful. The scorners are atheists. The atheist, not only denies God, but he exhibits antagonism and a hatred of God. They are the ones who are absolutely opposed to God. They don't want the Bible read in the public schools; they don't want it read anywhere for the matter. They deny the Word of God. There is nothing lower than to deny God. The drunkard in the gutter today is not nearly as low as the man who denies God. And if you want to know God's attitude, here it is: *"Surely He scorns the scornful, but He gives grace to the humble or lowly" (Proverbs 3:34).*

Psychology and Biblical Counseling

Secular psychology is based on the teachings of psychoanalysts such as Sigmund Freud, Carl Jung and Carl Rogers. Biblical counseling, on the other hand, is based squarely on the revealed Word of God. Biblical counseling sees Scripture as sufficient to equip the child of God for every good work (2 Timothy 3:17). Biblical counselors teach that man's basic problem is spiritual in nature; therefore, atheistic psychologists, who are spiritually dead themselves, have no real insight into the human condition.

In relationship, what is usually called "Christian counseling" is different from "Biblical counseling" in that Christian counseling often uses secular psychology in addition to the Bible. This is not to say that a Christian counselor is not also a biblical counselor, but often Christian counselors are Christians who integrate secular psychology into their counseling. Biblical counselors reject secular psychology.

Most psychology is humanistic in nature. Secular humanism promotes man and rejects the supernatural, faith and the Bible. Secular Psychology is man's attempt to understand and repair the spiritual side of man without reference to or recognition of the spiritual. ______**Recommended Resource:** Competent to Counsel by Jay Adams

While there may be some Christian psychologists who use only Scripture in their counseling, their designation of themselves as "Psychologists" is unfortunate. That word has an established meaning, which can only create confusion by the prestige it seems to award a godless system that does not merit any association with Christianity at all. There are also Christian psychologists who practice almost every type or kind of psychology and therapy designed. Therefore, godless beliefs and practices have been brought into the church. In order to return to Biblical Christianity, the church must cleanse itself of psychological theories and terminology and instead of accepting psychology as an additional source of truth, which Christ said God's Word alone is *"the truth"* (John 17:17).

***

Dr. Lawrence LeShan, PH.D, a clinical psychologist and parapsychologist, educator and author, also a past president of the Association for Humanistic Psychology, has suggested that "psychotherapy may be known as the hoax of the twentieth century." He went on to say, "As for psychiatrists diagnosing an illness predicated on something like pain and suffering or behavior or conduct is absurd to me and I would discount the diagnosis as much as I would distrust their theories of physical or chemical lobotomies or shock treatment." **[Posted in the Psychiatry Forum 'Psychiatry vs. Psychology' of Topix – July 9, 2016]**

What is Truth?

What is meant by truth is seldom considered. What we need to understand is: "All truth is God's truth" and in John 17: 17, Jesus says, *"Sanctify them by Your truth, Your Word is truth."*

"Psychotherapy deals with a subject upon which God has spoken with finality and about which He claims to have communicated in His Word the whole truth. There are no parts of this truth missing from the Bible and left to be discovered among the theories of the ungodly." ______ **(Dave Hunt, The Berean Call, July 2002)**

The Apostle Paul wrote, *"...no one knows the things of God except the Spirit of God" (1 Corinthians 2:11).* Paul is referring not to natural but to spiritual truths, which he specifically states are revealed by God only to true believers. We are told in no uncertain terms _____ *"But the natural man (unbeliever) does not receive the things of the Spirit of God, for they are foolishness to him; nor can he know them, because they are spiritually discerned" (1 Corinthians 2:14).* Furthermore, how can "God's truth" be communicated to humanists who have rejected even the witness of Creation and conscience? According to the Bible the only "truth" from God that the unbeliever can understand is that he is a sinner and needs a Savior. Until he is born again of the Spirit of God through faith in Christ, he cannot understand the "things of God" that are "spiritually discerned." It is only such, Paul declares, who *"have the mind of Christ"* (1 Corinthians 2:16). To the unsaved, Jesus said, *"He who is of God hears God's words; therefore you do not hear, because you are not of God" (John 8:47).*

In essence, there is enough Biblical and scientific evidence to close both the secular psychology, as well as the Christian Psychology platforms completely down. But the chance of that taking place is probably zero, in that the majority of Christians support such. This is due to factual evidence that most Christians fail to see the Bible as being the final authority of God's Word. What's better than best or better than perfection? Then why would Contemporary Christianity embrace psychology and psychotherapy in order to more effectively address a Christian's problems of living.

Perhaps the most difficult thought for our natural Egotism to entertain is that God **does not** need our help.

The author of this book theoretically believes most people, including Christians, suffer from such high self-esteem, along with Christian Psychologists (supported by their titles), that a balance cannot be achieved without first looking to the following Scriptures from God's Word:

<u>**Galatians 2:20**</u>, *"I have been crucified with Christ; it is no longer I who live, but Christ lives in me; and the life which I now live in the flesh I live by faith in the Son of God, who loved me and gave Himself for me."*

<u>**Galatians 5:24**</u>, *"And those who are Christ's have crucified the flesh with its passions and desires."*

* * *

"Never allow your ego to diminish your ability to listen."

– **Gary Hopkins**

"Ego is the anesthesia that deadens the pain of stupidity."

– **Rick Rigsby**

Questions for Personal Evaluation or Group Discussion

Chapter 6

1. Should psychology be placed on the same level as God's Word?

2. What do you think of when you consider the word church?

3. Read Acts 20:17-38; this explains that the church of God was purchased with His own blood. We become a member of His church when we receive Salvation.

Notes

Interim Chapter

(Written in the 1st Person)

"Only God fully appreciates the influence of a Christian Mother in the molding of character in her children."

– Billy Graham

★★★

It is with great pride and in humble adoration that I pause in the middle of this book to offer a keen and well deserved acknowledgment of my mother, Eugenia Mildred Pirkle.

I am most privileged to have learned and gleaned at her feet while growing up. Through her example, both her teaching and her exemplary life style, I was able to receive a far more advanced education than I could have in any institution of higher learning.

She was born in Dallas, Texas, moved to Chicago at age six, attended a high profile Catholic school through the eighth grade and received many awards in scholastics. She was an accomplished musician and a track star during her school years. Later, she met my Dad, who was in the ministry, and used her musical talent in the church. Being the youngest of four siblings, I recall my mother playing the piano, accordion, an old pump organ, guitar and mandolin, just a wonderful musician. She also had an extremely beautiful voice and knew how to read music from the old school of music. More than anything else, she was a dedicated child of God who studied her Bible and prayed daily. She always had a desire to help others and a sincere love and compassion for mankind.

In all my years while growing up, I never saw her sleep late or go to bed early; in fact I only recall seeing her in bed, due to sickness, prior to my sixteenth birthday. She only had two or three dresses to work around the house in and she would wash the one she took off at the end of the day and get up the next morning and iron it. She was one of the finest cooks, always preparing fine meals for our family. During my childhood, the Blue Law was in effect and there were no stores open on Sunday, so she would prepare our Sunday meals on Saturday. Often times, we would have company after church on Sunday at our home, in which she would serve sometimes as many as sixteen people. During those years, I recall well-known singers, such as the "Happy Goodmans", the "Spear Family", George Younce of the "Cathedrals," the "LeFevres," the "Hemphills" and various singers that have and are still appearing with Bill and Gloria Gaither, joining my family for Sunday dinner.

It was not unusual to see my mother cutting grass with an old rotary push mower or painting when I returned home from school. She always was a fantastic house keeper, and kept things in our home nice and maintained a warm and homey atmosphere. She sewed and made her own clothes, Crocheted, tatted, knitted, quilted and was very artistic. We were not financially well to do, but she always made pies and food to share with the sick, as well as elderly shut-ins. She never failed to offer words of wisdom from the Bible and prayer to those in need. She was loved by everyone I ever met and had a great heart of compassion for people in general.

Her penmanship was superb. While I was in Vietnam, she would write very encouraging letters (3 or 4 per week) and send them to me, even though I wouldn't receive them for sometimes three weeks or a month after she mailed them. She prayed earnestly every day and I knew it. When I got discharged from the military and returned home, she was waiting at the mailbox, which was fifty feet out from our house, with open arms.

Her personality and cooking could make anyone well that was sick. I never heard her complain or get angry. She was not self-centered or ever mentioned her birthday or ever asked for something special. She never forgot to express delight or failed to remember family and friend's birthdays. By the time I was in the seventh grade I knew hundreds of hymns, choruses and spiritual songs due to her singing and living the example before me. I grew up thinking we were rich (and we were), but not in a monetary way, but rich in faith in God, hope and love. She is the only one I can ever remember that could make a five dollar bill, during the 1960s, stretch into the equivalence of a twenty dollar bill.

We live in a very self-centered world today that is selfish and lazy, not to speak of those who are graduating from colleges and universities that cannot even write, do simple math in their head and communicate in a thorough, simple fashion. While television and Hollywood have become a liability in our society that has directly and indirectly changed our thinking, God has not and will never change.

I remember my mother requiring all us children to line our clothes on hangers faced to the right in our closet, as well as our shoes had to be polished on Saturday evenings by 8:30 and aligned beneath our hanging clothes in the closet. We were trained to get our bath and get to bed at a reasonable hour, so as to arise early on Sunday morning and prepare ourselves for Sunday school and church.

Every evening we had Scripture reading and prayer before going to bed. We always gave thanks to God for our food and were taught to eat every bite of food that was upon our plate. No one was excused from the table until all had finished.

The first television did not come out until I was in the second grade, which had a 12" black and white screen with tubes in the back. We didn't get a TV until I was in the 5th grade and I was allowed to watch Hop-Along Cassidy or Roy Rogers for a half hour after school, unless we went outside and played football or some other sport.

My mother was the most industrious and yet the most talented person I have ever seen, and to be so gracious and accommodating at the same time. Her life was the greatest living testimony I have ever seen and the only reason I would want her back in this present world is for selfish reasons. In Proverbs 31:26-31, we read, She opens her mouth with wisdom, and on her tongue is the law of kindness. She watches over the ways of her household, and does not eat the bread of idleness. Her children rise up and call her blessed; her husband also, and he praises her: "many daughters have done well, but you excel them all." Charm is deceitful and beauty is passing, but a woman who fears the Lord, she shall be praised. Give her of the fruit of her hands, and let her own works praise her in the gates. May I leave this with you, as it reminds me of my mother's advice throughout my early years:

There's **No Storm** that God
won't carry you through.
No Bridge that God won't
help you cross.
No battle that God won't help you win. **No**
heartache that God won't help you let go of.
He is SO much bigger than
anything you will face today.
Leave everything in His Hands
And embrace this day confidently knowing
that He WILL take care of you.

WordPress.com

CHAPTER

VII

"Caution!"

THINK WHILE IT'S STILL LEGAL

Are you a robot?

Yes or No

(How much knowledge and wisdom did you receive from this Blank Page?)

You will achieve the same by failing to read the Bible, God's Word.

Warnings

A Guard Rail or railing is a system designed to keep people or vehicles from (in most cases unintentionally) straying into dangerous or off-limits areas.

These boundaries are placed there to keep us from heading to areas we don't want to go. They only alert us, but they do not necessarily keep us from going through or over them. Boundaries are critical in our everyday lives, especially in our spiritual life. If we want to pursue integrity and properly reflect God's character, we need personal boundaries. In Proverbs 22:3 we read, *"A prudent man foresees evil and hides himself, but the simple pass on and are punished."* A prudent man is a wise, sensible or a well advised person. There are some Scriptural guardrails in the Bible (Basic Instructions Before Leaving Earth) which we all need to examine and establish in our lives, such as Ephesians 5:15-17, *"See then that you walk circumspectly, not as fools but as wise, redeeming the time, because the days are evil."* mentioned in the Bible, that of Adam and Eve. In Genesis 2:8 we read, *"The Lord God planted a garden eastward of Eden, and there He put the man whom He had formed."* It goes on to say in verses 15-17, *"Then the Lord God took the man and put him in the Garden of Eden to tend and keep it. And the Lord God commanded the man, saying, Of every tree of the garden, you may freely eat; but of the tree of the knowledge of good and evil you shall not eat, for in the day that you eat of it, you shall surely die."* In the next few verses of chapter 2, we read God didn't want man to be alone, so He made the man a helper, comparable to him, by taking a rib from Adam in which he made a woman and joined her to Adam, as his wife. In verse 25, it says, *"And they were both naked, the man and his wife, and were not ashamed"* (naked here meaning there was no sin). Chapter 3 reveals the details of the lie of the serpent when he confronted the woman in the garden concerning the fruit of the tree of the knowledge of good and evil. After she ate of the fruit and gave to her husband and he ate, verse 7 says, *"Then the eyes of both of them were opened, and they knew that they were naked* (aware of their sin); *and they sowed fig leaves together and made themselves coverings."* Verse 8 says, *"And they heard the sound of the Lord God walking in the garden in the cool of the day, and Adam and his wife hid themselves from the presence of the Lord God among the trees of the garden."* In verses 9-24, God asked Adam, *"Who told you that you were naked?"* After God questioned Adam about them eating from the forbidden tree, He cursed the serpent, and then explained to the woman that He would greatly multiply her sorrow and her conception; and she would be in pain as she brought forth children. God cursed the ground and told Adam that man would have to toil or work all the days of his life. Then God drove them out of the Garden of Eden.

In Genesis 3:21, it says God made coats of skins and clothed them. In order to have the skins of animals, the animals have to be killed or slain. This is the origin of sacrifice. God rejected their fig leaves, but made them clothing of skins. This offers four great lessons from the fig leaves, according to **Through the Bible with J. Vernon McGee.** (1) Man must have adequate covering to approach God. You cannot come to God on the basis of your good works. You must come just as you are – a sinner. (2) Fig leaves are unacceptable; God does not take a homemade garment. (3) God must provide the covering. (4) The covering is obtained only through the death of the Lord Jesus. Salvation comes when you and I take our proper place as sinners before God.

Who lied to YOU? And why did YOU believe it? It had to have been Satan, who we refer to as the devil. The devil never uses devices such as painting pictures of pain and poverty, but rather that of great wealth, beauty, popularity and that which is appealing like power. Satan is still using the same plan today as he used in the Garden of Eden. When Jesus was speaking to the descendents of Abraham in John 8:31-47, He said in verse 44, *"...the devil is a liar and the father of it."* And as He speaks in First Peter 5:8, *"Be sober, be vigilant; because your adversary the devil walks about like a roaring lion, seeking whom he may devour."*

Guard Rails

Remember, guardrails are needed **BEFORE** sin. Ephesians 5:18-20, *"And do not be drunk with wine, in which is dissipation; but be filled with the Spirit, speaking to one another in psalms and hymns and spiritual songs,* *singing and making melody in your heart to the Lord, giving thanks always for all things to God the Father in the name of our Lord Jesus Christ."*

Often more than not, television shows, news reports, even sports broadcasts, tend to illustrate the sins in our world. Romans 12:2, *"And do not be conformed to this world, but be transformed by the renewing of your mind, that you may prove what is that good and acceptable and perfect will of God."*

We need to think on good things, those things that are of good substance, uplifting, wholesome, and things that will benefit our family and friends. A Psalm of David that has often been used as a prayer can direct our thinking and is found in Psalm 19:14, *"Let the words of my mouth and the meditation of my heart be acceptable in Your sight, O Lord, my strength and my Redeemer."* This prayer can be beneficial at work or at home, in meetings and in solitude, at play or while on a vacation, in every situation since it offers all the glory to God. Positive thinking won't get the job done but it will allow you to do everything better than negative thinking will. We need good guard rails to help eliminate "**Stinking Thinking**". We all need guard rails to help us stay on the right course. Besides the Bible, we need a church family to offer prayer support and mature fellowship to keep us sharp. This promotes team effort in a unified manner to help each other from becoming likened to an 'ingrown toe nail'. We have no idea what God has in store for our future. We could miss His Will for our life, by not setting up healthy personal boundaries.

Precautionary Warnings

Sometimes during athletic games, players are given a stern warning from the referee. Health warnings are placed on various packages for our own benefit and safety. The Bible offers many precautionary warnings in respect to our behavior.

Note: *Unless otherwise indicated, the information in this section is taken from the National Institute on Drug Abuse, Public Health Service, U.S. Dept. Of Health and Human Services*________________

[2/3 of American kids try an illegal drug before they finish high school. The leading cause of death at ages 15-24 is drunk driving. Many forces influence people, especially young people, to begin drug use. Much modern music, movies, and TV programs glorify illegal drugs, such as marijuana. It is openly promoted at concerts, on CDs, even on clothes – sending teens a message of social acceptance.]

<u>Below is a short-list of problems we manufacture</u>:

Addiction – Not a disease, but mainly coming from an over- indulgence of anything.

Greed – Jesus said to them, *"Take heed and beware of covetousness (greed), for one's life does not consist in the abundance of the things he possesses" (Luke 12:15).*

Hatred – <u>1 John 2:9</u>, *"He, who says he is in the light, and hates his brother, is in darkness until now."* <u>Proverbs 10:12</u>, *"Hatred stirs up strife, but love covers all offenses."* God hates Sin, **<u>not</u>** Sinners. Peter says, *"The Lord is not slack concerning His promise, as some count slackness, but is longsuffering toward us, not willing that any should perish but that all should come to repentance"(2 Peter 3:9).* Jesus said in <u>John</u> <u>15:18</u>, *"If the world hates you, you know that it hated Me before it hated you."*

Envy – <u>James 3:14-16</u>, *"But if you have bitter envy and self-seeking in your hearts, do not boast and lie against the truth. This wisdom does not descend from above, but is earthly, sensual, and demonic. For where envy and self-seeking exist, confusion and every evil thing are there."* <u>1 Corinthians 13:4</u>, *"Love suffers long and is kind; love does not envy, is not puffed up..."*

***

"When in doubt, leave it out"

Lying – <u>Proverbs 12:22</u>, *"Lying lips are an abomination to the Lord, but those who deal truthfully are His delight."*

Profanity – Exodus 20:7, *"You shall not take the name of the Lord your God in vain, for the Lord will not hold him guiltless who takes His name in vain."* Matthew 12:36-37, *"But I say to you that for every idle word men may speak, they will give account of it in the day of judgment. For by your words you will be justified, and by your words you will be condemned."*

Thievery – Ephesians 4:28, *"Let him who stole steal no longer, but rather let him labor, working with his hands what is good, that he may have something to give him who has need."*

Obsession – 1 John 2:15-17, *"Do not love the world or the things in the world. If anyone loves the world, the love of the Father is not in him. For all that is in the world – the lust of the flesh, the lust of the eyes, and the pride of life – is not of the Father but is of the world. And the world is passing away, and the lust of it; but he who does the will of God abides forever."*

Note: In case you think something has been left out of the above list, please know it is inclusive in the following passage of Scripture.

"Now the works of the flesh are evident, which are: adultery, fornication, uncleanness, lewdness, idolatry, sorcery, hatred, contentions, jealousies, outbursts of wrath, selfish ambitions, dissensions, heresies, envy, murders, drunkenness, revelries, and the like, of which I tell you beforehand, just as I also told you in time past, that those who practice such things will not inherit the kingdom of God" (Galatians 5:19-24).

Bad Habits

"The cure for boredom is curiosity. The only cure for curiosity is through researching factually based truth."

While there are large numbers of people who are simply bored, there are others who form bad habits from dealing with stress and boredom. Things such as biting finger nails to going on shopping sprees to binge drinking on weekends to wasting time on the internet.

Nevertheless, while those who are curiously seeking, are usually doing so in search of all the wrong things in all the wrong places. Bad habits tend to interrupt our lives and prevent us from accomplishing our goals, if we have any. They also tend to jeopardize our health, mentally and physically. Quite often, they waste our time and energy.

First of all, we can't stop bad habits, we can only replace them. If we are a Christian, the Bible *(Basic Instructions before Leaving Earth)* is the best source of help we can find. We read in Jeremiah 29:13, *"And you will seek Me and find Me, when you search for Me with all your heart."* And in Romans 12:2, *"And do not be conformed to this present world, but be transformed by the renewing of your mind, that you may prove what is that good and acceptable and perfect will of God."*

A Short List of Expensive Habits

Smoking Cigarettes – The average person that smokes absorbs the cost of $2600. Per year, not to speak of lung cancer.

Chewing Tobacco – The average cost is $900. per year. There are over 30 different cancer-causing agents in chewing tobacco. It usually doesn't make it to the lungs, but the mouth, throat, cheek, gums, lips, jaw or chin has increased possibilities. Pancreatic cancer and kidney cancer are likely.

Alcoholic Beverages – According to the Washington Post, almost 30% of the country never touches alcohol, and another 30% do so only on special occasions, or every couple of weeks. The highest on the chart take about 73 drinks a week. People who drink heavily have a greater risk of liver disease, heart disease, sleep disorders, depression, stroke, bleeding from the stomach, sexually transmitted infections from unsafe sex, and several types of cancer. They may have problems managing diabetes, high blood pressure, and other conditions. Drinking during pregnancy can cause brain damage and other serious problems, such as birth defects. ___**Rethinking Drinking**

Note: The best way to not become addicted to alcohol is to refrain from taking the first drink.

How Destructive is Satan?

Satan is cunning and crafty. He is also more powerful than we give him credit for and one to be guarded against. If the temptations of this world and the sin within our own hearts aren't enough, just remember Satan is working overtime to see our destruction. He has all kinds of evil on his side plus the fact that he never grows tired and never gives up throwing his hatred against Christ and His bride. He has no compassion and he doesn't care how hard life is for you or the things you have gone through. He rejoices in our difficulties and constantly wants to add to them.

Another thing Satan loves to do is to plant doubts in our heart by posing the question, "How can a good God possibly let such horrible things happen to us?"

> "Hell is the highest reward that the devil can offer you for being a servant of his."
>
> – **Billy Sunday**

> "We must recognize how the evil one is working in this world and take a firm stance against him. It means we take careful thought concerning what we put in our minds – what we listen to, what we watch, and how we use our time."
>
> – **Chip Ingram**

Remember – "Good Habits are just as hard to break as bad habits."

Questions for Personal Evaluation or Group Discussion

Chapter 7

1. How can warnings and guard rails be beneficial according to God's Word?

2. What scriptures deal with conformity to the world and bad thinking?

3. Is drug addiction the only addiction in our world?

4. Discuss several ways that illustrate Satan's destructive force.

Notes

CHAPTER VIII

"The Biblical View of Death"

The best News in the World comes from the Christian perspective. There is no way you can live the Christian life properly without first understanding the Biblical perspective on death.

A wife said to her husband, "Shall we watch the six o'clock news and get indigestion or wait for the eleven o'clock and have insomnia?" Someone else put it, "The evening news is where they begin with 'Good evening' – and then tell you why it isn't." The world's picture of "Death" is so absurd that it is apparent they are only studying Fiction books or living in an imaginary Dream world. We live in a world filled with tragedy and if there's anything this world needs is Good News.

You perhaps are thinking why then are you sharing this study on death. No one likes to even discuss such a word. They want to think they can extend their life span as long as possible. This is understandable to the unbeliever, but not to the 'Born Again' child of God. *Since Christ, who will never die, lives in believers, and since He has promised to never leave us, then we can never go to hell.* Christ's life assures us of Eternal Salvation. Therefore, the Christian can say along with the Apostle Paul in Philippians 1:21, *"For to me, to live is Christ, and to die is gain."* This is why we sing that wonderful old hymn of the church -- "Blessed Assurance, Jesus is Mine..."

As has often been stated, a person is not ready to live unless he is ready to die. To live properly, we must live purposely. We should always notice in our rearview mirror, the certainty of death and the uncertainty of when it will occur. We must be aware it could take place at any moment.

Death

How many times have you heard someone say, "We'll all live till we die?" The one principle we should all have permeating our minds is the certainty of death. Someone said, "Life is like a roll of toilet paper – the closer you get to the end, the more quickly it goes." The Bible says in Genesis 2:7, *"And the Lord God formed man of the dust of the ground, and breathed into his nostrils the breath of life; and man became a living soul."* Genesis 3:19, *"In the sweat of your face you shall eat bread till you return to the ground, for out of it you were taken; for dust you are, and to dust you shall return."* Psalm 103:14, *"For He knows our frame; He remembers that we are dust."* Psalm 90:12, *"So teach us to number our days, that we may gain a heart of wisdom."*

Is there life after death?

Though we may die, Jesus says, *"I am the resurrection and the life. He who believes in Me, though he may die, he shall live" (John 11:25)*. There is Life for the children of God. We will receive immortality when Jesus comes again (see 1 Corinthians 15:51-54). The Bible says that all those who have died – both righteous and wicked – will be raised in one of two resurrections. The righteous will be raised to life at Jesus' second coming. *"For the Lord Himself will descend from heaven with a shout, with the voice of an archangel, and with the trumpet of God. And the dead in Christ will rise first" (1 Thessalonians 4:16)*. According to this verse, the righteous do not go to heaven when they die. They remain asleep in the grave until Jesus returns and raises them to immortal life (see 1 Corinthians 15:50-57).

The wicked are raised to life in a separate resurrection – the resurrection of condemnation. Jesus said, *"Do not marvel at this; for the hour is coming in which all who are in the graves will hear His voice and come forth – those who have done good, to the resurrection of life, and those who have done evil, to the resurrection of condemnation" (John 5:28-29).* Neither did Jesus nor His apostles teach that the righteous immediately go to heaven or the wicked go to hell when they die. Prior to Jesus leaving His disciples, He did not tell them they would join Him soon. However, He did say in John 14:1-3, *"Let not your heart be troubled; you believe in God, believe also in Me. In my Father's house are many mansions; if it were not so, I would have told you. I go to prepare a place for you. And if I go and prepare a place for you, I will come again and receive you to Myself; that where I am, there you may be also."*

Just imagine like the song – *"What a Day That Will be"*, – when He returns, the righteous ones shall awake from their tombs. No matter how long time has passed, it will seem but a moment to them. Jesus will call them and they will awaken to a wonderful and glorious immortality.

"For the trumpet will sound, and the dead will be raised incorruptible... So when this corruptible has put on incorruption, and this mortal has put on immortality, then shall be brought to pass the saying that is written: "O Death, where is your sting? O Hades, where is your victory?" (1 Corinthians 15:55).

Fear Sin, NOT Death

In that God appears at time's beginning is not too difficult to comprehend, but that He appears at the beginning and end of time simultaneously is not easy to realize; yet it is true. We understand **Time** by a succession of events. Changes do not take place all at once, but rather in succession, one after the other. Since we read in Romans 3:23, *"For all have sinned and fall short of the glory of God"*, it is imperative that we also read Psalm 90:12, *"So teach us to number our days, that we may gain a heart of wisdom."* In other words, we are to realize the brevity of life and in doing so we may develop wisdom in our hearts. Fear does not come from God, but rather love. 1 John 4:18, 19, reveals *"There is no fear in love; but perfect love casts out fear, because fear involves torment. But he who fears has not been made perfect in love. We love Him because He first loved us."*

> "Fear is born of Satan, and if we would only take time to think a moment we would see that everything Satan says is founded upon a falsehood."
>
> – A.B. Simpson

The minute we accept Christ Jesus, as our Savior and Lord we begin to live and at that moment we need to read the words of the Apostle Paul found in Galatians 2:20, *"I have been crucified with Christ; it is no longer I who live, but Christ lives in me; and the life which I now live in the flesh I live by faith in the Son of God, who loved me and gave himself for me."* And Jesus said in Luke 9:23, *"If anyone desires to come after Me, let him deny himself, and take up his cross daily,* (means to die to self daily) *and follow Me."* Continue in verses 24-26____ *"For whoever desires to save his life will lose it, but whoever loses his life for My sake will save it. For what profit is it to a man if he gains the whole world, and is himself destroyed or lost? For whoever is ashamed of Me and My words, of him the Son of Man will be ashamed when He comes in His own glory, and in His Father's, and of the holy angels."*

Someone said, "How sweet the name of Jesus sounds, in a believer's ear. It soothes his sorrows, heals his wounds, and drives away his fear."

The Second Death

The second death is mentioned various times in the book of Revelation and is synonymous with the lake of fire. It is called the "second" death because it follows physical death. This death is a separation from God, the Giver of Life. Revelation 21:8 makes it very clear in that it says, *"But the cowardly, unbelieving, abominable, murderers, sexually immoral, sorcerers, idolaters, and all liars shall have their part in the lake which burns with fire and brimstone, which is the second death."* Physical death is a one-time experience. Eternal death, on the other hand, is everlasting. It is a death that continues eternally, a spiritual death that is experienced on a continual basis. Just as spiritual life is everlasting life, eternal death is never-ending.

God's Word, the Bible, is the infallible rule of faith, and this we must believe and teach since it definitely teaches eternal death. Three passages, one in the Old Testament and two in the New are: Daniel 12:2 *"And many of those who sleep in the dust of the earth shall awake, some to everlasting life, some to shame and everlasting contempt."* Matthew 25:46 *"And these will go away into everlasting punishment, but the righteous into eternal life."* Revelation20:15 *"And anyone not found in the Book of Life was cast into the lake of fire."* In verse 10, it reads that the "Lake of Fire" burns forever and ever.

The doctrine of eternal death is not a popular doctrine to proclaim. However, we should not refrain from such, since the Bible clearly teaches it, and we were born in sin and trespasses, and fall under the just condemnation of God for our sin. The Bible teaches that except we accept the saving message of Jesus Christ, we will perish and fall under God's judgment, which is --- eternal death. This is why such teaching should be offered or presented with the utmost care and compassion.

The Spiritually Dead

All mankind born after the fall in the Garden of Eden inherited a sin nature and therefore are spiritually stillborn. We read in Psalm 51:5 *"Behold, I was brought forth in iniquity, and in sin my mother conceived me."* To be spiritually dead does not mean to be without the intellectual faculties. Our minds, emotions and wills still function, but they are cut off from the life of God. The best way to understand spiritual death is that our souls are separated from God. Sin separates us from God. The spiritually dead sit in darkness and have no spiritual life or light in God's Word. The penalty for sin is death (Romans 3:23). To be spiritually dead means to be insensitive to the things of God and ignorant of spiritual thinking according to (1 Corinthians 2:14). A spiritually dead person does not love God and cannot please Him. They want to please themselves instead of God --- *"For all seek their own, not the things which are of Christ Jesus" (Philippians 2:21).* Though Scripture gives us a picture of what it means to be spiritually dead, it is not a pretty one.

Because of God's great love, He sent His only Begotten Son, Jesus Christ, who is the Resurrection and the Life, into this dark world to die for us. Many times churches nowadays seek to become bigger, flashier, and more technologically savvy. They usually tend to become more cold and impersonal. A lot of Contemporary churches seem to encourage the "me first" or the "self-love" agenda, rather than following the Scripture, which encourages us to love one another. In Galatians 5:14 Paul admonished the Galatian churches to love and serve one another when he said, *"For all the law is fulfilled in one word, even in this: You shall love your neighbor as yourself."*

"Love is Not Selfish"

"The Bridge"

There is a bridge you can take,
it leads to water's living...
It's there you'll find peace
merciful and forgiving.

Over trials and tribulations,
it will take you across
the span of His loving hands
will lead you to the Cross

It is a bridge of assurance
troubled waters will not last
and for you He has a future
much better than the past.

The hardships in this life,
will take faith to get through
and Jesus is the bridge linking
His Father right to you!
By Deborah Ann Belka

"The more I help others, the more I succeed"

What Does It Mean to Die to Self?

Romans 6:8 *"Now if we died with Christ, we believe that we shall also live with Him."*

Jesus described the *"dying to self"* process or "denying self" as part of following Him. ---- *"If anyone desires to come after Me, let him deny himself, and take up his cross, and follow Me" (Matthew 16:24);* He then went on to say that *"dying to self"* is actually a positive, not a negative: *"For whoever desires to save his life will lose it, but whoever loses his life for My sake will find it" (Matthew 16:25).* In dying to the self-life, we discover an abundant life by depending on God, who provides much more than we can imagine. Jesus put it this way: *"Unless a grain of wheat falls into the ground and dies, it remains alone; but if it dies, it produces much grain" (John 12:24).* Part of the life we discover when we give our lives to Christ, is freedom from a life of self-obsession and we experience the joy of Christ, and become more accepting, generous and loving of others. We then set aside our wants and desires, and start to focus on loving God, and valuing others as much as we value ourselves. Dying to ourselves is something most people find hard to do. Dying to self is an ongoing process, seeking His will and kingdom, rather than our own. It is an integral part of the process of sanctification. Dying to self is never seen as optional in Scripture. As believers we are to take up our cross daily and follow Christ. It is our "daily cross" that causes us to cry out like Jesus, *"Father, why is this?"*...that gives us a longing for heaven. Paul said, *"...I die daily (1 Corinthians 15:31).*

The goal of death to self is Fellowship with Christ. As A.W. Tozer would say, reject the praise of men, embrace simplicity and child-like faith. Dying to self is no easy task. As long as we are on this earth, we have the flesh to contend with.

★★★

Some Noteworthy Quotes

Martin Luther – *"Until a man is nothing, God can make nothing out of him."*

Richard Sibbes – *"Self-emptiness prepares us for spiritual fullness."*

Ignatius – *"Few souls understand what God would accomplish in them if they were to abandon themselves unreservedly to Him."*

Vance Havner – *"Some missionaries bound for Africa were laughed at by the boat captain who said, "You'll only die over there." Replied a missionary: "Captain, we died before we started."*

Will Suicide Send You to Hell?

Many people have asked this question and there has been much discussion about it, but this is not something that this author can easily give an absolute answer to. However, murder is called the ultimate attack upon the image of God, in that God created us in His own image, according to Genesis 9:6. If we were to read in Romans 14:23, we would note Paul saying, *"...for whatever is not from faith is sin."* Therefore, if we were to violate a conviction that God has placed in our heart, clearly, it is sin. We should not want to take a chance of violating the image of God in us, since it is the ultimate act of the lack of faith and without faith it is impossible to please God. None of us should want to meet God on those terms.

One of the most difficult moments a pastor or counselor could experience is confronting a parent or close relatives whose dealing with someone who has taken their own life.

This is a time we need to know that God is not naïve to our grief and pain, and it is in the middle of these hard realities, that we can point them to Christ through His words in 2nd Corinthians 12:9 – *"My grace is sufficient for you, for My strength is made perfect in weakness."*

Friend, if you are reading this book and you have entertained thoughts of ending your life, stop and realize this is a trick of Satan. He is a liar and a deceiver, while God who created you is the way, the truth and the life. Call on Him at this very moment and put your trust in Jesus Christ, the only begotten Son of God. Only He and He alone can offer you the peace that passes all understanding.

Someone said, "Pain is inevitable, suffering is optional."

Remember – Jesus Christ is the only answer.

Questions for Personal Evaluation or Group Discussion

Chapter 8

1. Physical death is when the body ceases to function, no matter what our status in life, rich or poor, young or old. This is why Jesus came to earth and died, that we might have life after death. Why should we fear sin, not death?

2. What is the Second Death?

3. Consider what is meant by dying to self and sanctification.

Notes

CHAPTER

"Wealth"

> *"God does not need your money. He wants what it represents – You. While God supplies our finances, He desires us to prioritize His work in giving. He wants us to purpose to follow Him no matter what happens with our finances."*
>
> –Jack Hyles

Do you spend more time thinking about money than you do thinking on the things of God? If your answer is yes you may need to take a look at your priorities. As a Christian nothing should be more important nor consume your thoughts and actions more than your relationship with the Lord. Everything you think and do should be to His glory. *"Let the words of my mouth, and the meditation of my heart, be acceptable in Your sight, O Lord, my strength, and my redeemer" (Psalm 19:14).*

Frequently Asked Questions

1. Why hasn't God answered my prayers to get out of debt?
2. Why do people have money problems, even when they are serving God?

3. Will God make me prosperous and wealthy?
4. Where in the Bible does it say God will prosper me?

The Bible Does not Promise Wealth. There is no promise in the Bible that being a Christian will lead to a good job, wealth, or freedom from debt etc.

God's faithful people may be rich or poor as seen throughout the Scriptures – Mark 12:41-44 *Now Jesus sat opposite the treasury and saw how the people put money into the treasury. And many who were rich put in much. Then one poor widow came and threw in two mites, which make a quadrans (equal to a quarter). So He called His disciples to Himself and said to them, "Assuredly, I say to you that this poor widow has put in more than all those who have given to the treasury; for they all put in out of their abundance, but she out of her poverty put in all that she had, her whole livelihood."* Proverbs 22:2 reads, *"The rich and the poor have this in common, the Lord is the maker of them all."*

The ideal rich man in the Bible was Job. He never loved his wealth more than God. He used it freely to help others. He was introduced as an exceptionally prosperous man (Job 1:3). He had seven sons and three daughters according to (Job 1:3). Job believed his success to be the result of God's blessing. In (Job 1:10) we are told God has *"blessed the work of his hands, and his possessions have increased in the land."* In verse 1, while we see Job as being "blameless and upright", he seems to worry that his children may inadvertently sin against God. So after every feast Job would send and sanctify them and he would rise early in the morning and offer burnt offerings according to the number of them all. God recognizes Job's faithfulness to Satan one day when Satan came, at which time Satan said, *"Does Job fear God for nothing?"* (1:9). We could apply this question to ourselves. Do we relate to God primarily so that He will bless us with the material things we want? When times are good and we do in fact, prosper, it is natural to thank God for our wealth. The pain comes when times are hard. When we are passed over for promotion or lose a job. When we become chronically ill, or we lose someone we love, then what?

We may begin to face the question, "If God was blessing me during the good times, is He punishing me now." Satan hopes to set a trap for Job. Satan then says to God if you remove the blessings you have bestowed on Job, *"he will curse You to Your face!"* If Satan can get Job to think he is being punished by God, Job may be between a rock and a hard place. He may stop his righteous habits in the idea they are offensive to God, or perhaps thinking from the accuser's point of view, he will become bitter at God for his punishment and leave God altogether. Regardless, it will be a curse in the face of God. However, God allowed Satan to proceed. Nearly everything Job has is stolen and the people he loves, including his children are murdered or killed in storms (Job 1:13-16). But Job never thinks God is punishing him nor becomes bitter toward God. Instead he worships God in chapter 1, vs. 20. At his lowest moment, Job blesses God during all the circumstances of life, good or bad. *"The Lord gave, and the Lord has taken away; blessed be the name of the Lord" (Job 1:21).* Job has a balanced attitude and he understands his early prosperity was a blessing from God. He never thought he deserved God's blessing, even though he honored God. Neither does he think he deserves his current sufferings, necessarily. He doesn't really know why God blessed him with all the prosperity earlier and not at this time.

The "prosperity gospel" probably hates this passage. It claims that those in a right relationship with God are always blessed with prosperity (such as Joel Osteen). This is not true, and Job is proof. Job is also a rebuke to the "poverty gospel" which believes the opposite, in that a right relationship with God means a life of poverty.

As a result of Job enduring overwhelming loss without compromising, the Scripture says in Job 1:22, *"In this entire Job did not sin nor charge God with wrong."*

But Satan doesn't give up. God allows Satan to destroy Job's health (2:1-11). God even allows Satan to afflict Job *"with painful boils "from the sole of his foot to the crown of his head" (Job 2:7). Then his wife said to him, "Do you still hold fast to your integrity? Curse God and die!" But he said to her, "You speak as one of the foolish women speaks. Shall we indeed accept good from God, and shall we not accept adversity?" In all this Job did not sin with his lips (verses 9-10).*

Again we find Job attributing every circumstance of life to God. He is totally unaware of what God is doing in the heavenly activity concerning his situation. It is only the integrity of his faith that prevents him from cursing God. During good times do we practice faithfulness and thanksgiving in preparing for adversity? Job's unwavering habit of prayer and sacrifice perhaps seems unusual or even a little quirky when we encounter it in Job1:5. But now we can see a lifetime of faithful practices has paid off and allowed him to remain faithful in extreme circumstances. Faith in God may come in an instant, but integrity is formed over a lifetime.

From a Practical Standpoint

In most cases, we can realize that in the workplace when adversity arises, along with the loss of means of income, we can easily become so self-identified with our work that strain spreads to our family and personal lives. In most cases it plays havoc in not getting a good night's rest or even destruction of our family. In this passage of Scripture, we may even be tempted to draw a moral such as, "Don't get so wrapped up in your work that its problems affect your family or your health." However, this analogy wouldn't do justice to the depth of Job's story. Job's problems did affect his family and his health, in addition to his work. This story is about Job's wisdom in reference to maintaining faithfulness to God, rather than how to maintain wise boundaries. The world might say, having Faith in God is not practical. They're right, **God is not practical**, but Divine and sovereign. *"For as the heavens are higher than the earth, so are My ways than your ways, and My thoughts than your thoughts" (Isaiah 55:9)*. Job gave God all the glory through all the circumstances.

This is what most rich people fail in. They find it easy to say thanks when they are prospering and have plenty, but when so-called Christians (in name only) lose their wealth or health, they begin to doubt God's sovereign power. Everyone can seemingly love God when all things are going well for them.

The Bible deals a lot with riches. The ideal according to Proverbs is a middle amount of wealth. *"Remove falsehood and lies far from me; give me neither poverty or riches – Feed me with the food allotted to me; lest I be full and deny You, and say, Who is the Lord? Or lest I be poor and steal, and profane the name of my God" (Proverbs 30:8-9).*

The Apostle Paul wrote that he had learned how to be content with both poverty and abundance in (Philippians 4:12-13). Jesus had rich friends who helped support Him (Luke 8:3). He did not tell them to give all their money away and be poor.

Wealth, according to the Bible, is like fire, both good and yet dangerous. The Bible warns us about the danger. (1) The desire to get rich in (1 Timothy6:10). (2) Worry about money (Matthew 6:24). (3) Trusting in wealth rather than God (Luke 12:16-21). (4) Loving money as your god, when no man can actually serve two masters (Matthew 6:24). (5) Using your money to oppress other people (James 2:6). The goal of getting rich is a foolish goal. You can't take it with you (1 Timothy 6:7).

Unconditional Love

You may say what has wealth got to do with love. A great deal when you consider the Bible saying, *"the love of money is the root of all evil."* God is love and He hates evil. Let's take time to consider that although volumes have been written about the characteristics of God, the very nature of God is Love, Life and Holiness.

He is love (1John 4:8), He is life (Revelations 22:1) and He is holiness (Psalms 99:9). Love is the very essence of who He is. His life and holiness are an expression of His love. Love is not something He chooses to do or give. We should be thankful God's love is not like the love expressed by many in today's culture – a love of convenience and ego. Such as, "I'll love you as long as you please me and add value to my life or at which time my love for you will cease." This is conditional love.

The Unconditional love of God requires relationship and seeks expression and therefore, there must be an object of that love to make it complete.

God's love is revealed in that He created us in His own image and likeness. Part of that image/likeness is freedom of choice. We can choose to ignore or reject God's love or we can choose to accept and embrace His love. The life He gives us offers us the capacity and desire to be in relationship and to love in return. To live in God is to live in love (1 John 4:16).

For example, in order to establish communication, there must be a communicator and a communicatee so that there can be communication.

Our relationship with God must be one of intimacy and not just head knowledge. To put it simple, Love loves!

Salvation is based on God's love and mercy, not our worthiness. We read in Titus 3:4-5 *"But when the kindness and the love of God our Savior toward man appeared, not by works of righteousness which we have done, but according to His mercy He saved us, through the washing of regeneration and renewing of the Holy Spirit."*

Then out of response to Christ's offering on the Cross, we should follow through by drinking in Romans 12:1, *"I beseech you therefore, brethren, by the mercies of God, that you present your bodies a living sacrifice, holy, acceptable to God, which is your reasonable service."*

Note: To know God intimately opens the door for revelation and fulfillment. It brings change of essence, expression, behavior, desires, identity and security that no other knowledge offers. This is a key to how we should reason about everything.

A Summary of Job's Life

Earlier we had an opportunity to glean for a short moment in the early part of Job's life. We noted that God blessed him with a great business, a wonderful family (seven sons and three daughters), a remarkable influence upon those is his area, along with the proper understanding that God had blessed him and we note that Job constantly prayed to God and took no credit for any good in his life. Now as we advance further through the story of Job's life, we see God not only allows Satan to strip him of his wealth, but his health. It is during this period of his life we see Job's three friends – Eliphaz, Bildad and Zophar (Job 4-23) come and sit with Job for seven days, quietly at first, and then proceed to accuse him of doing evil. It seems we tend to want to give a reason for someone suffering, be it right or wrong, rather than accepting the mystery at the heart of the suffering. Sometimes people will say, "It's all for the best." "It's part of God's plan." "God never sends people more adversity than they can handle." How arrogant to imagine we know God's plan or think we know the reason for anyone else's suffering. Eliphaz even said, *"There is no end to your iniquities"* (Job 22:5).

Sometimes out of sheer laziness, bad info or incompetence, we make poor decisions that cause us to fail at work. Not all failures are the direct result of our own shortcomings, however. We should be careful not to misjudge others, as well as ourselves.

Job showed wisdom many of us, as Christians lack, in that he directed his emotions at God rather than at himself or those around him (Job 13:3, 23-24). Job knew only God had the answer and when he questioned God, he did so with the faith that God was the resource, but may not answer immediately or at all. However, Job was steadfast to God and did not waiver in his faithfulness.

It appeared at times the friends of Job were being used as tools of Satan, not God. We all know that the very demons of hell seem to plague us after failure. For example, Eliphaz said in the form of a question, *"Can a man be profitable to God, though he who is wise may be profitable to himself?"(Job 22:2). "Is not God in the height of heaven? And see the highest stars, how lofty they are!"(Job 22:12).* Job is not trying to blame God, but rather trying to learn from God. Regardless of how much God has permitted to afflict Job, Job knows God can use the experience to shape his soul for the better. Job realizes that God's wisdom is beyond his understanding. We read in Job 28:12-13, *"But where can wisdom be found? And where is the place of understanding? Man does not know its value, nor is it found in the land of the living."*

Job's Repentance and Restoration

Job the servant became Job the intercessor.

According to the Exposition Commentary by **Warren W. Wiersbe**, Job 42:1-6 -- Quote: "Job knew he was beaten. There was no way he could argue his case with God. Quoting God's very words (Job 42:3-4), Job humbled himself before the Lord and acknowledged His power and justice in executing His plans (v. 2). Then Job admitted that his words had been wrong and that he had spoken about things he didn't understand (v. 3). Job withdrew his accusations that God was unjust and not treating him fairly. He realized that whatever God does is right and man must accept by faith.

Job told God, "I can't answer Your questions! All I can do is confess my pride, humble myself, and repent." Until now, Job's knowledge of God had been indirect and impersonal; but that was changed. Job had met God personally and seen himself to be but "dust and ashes" (v. 6; 2:8, 12; Genesis 18:27).

"The door of repentance opens into the hall of joy," said Charles Spurgeon; and it was true for Job. In the climax of the book, Job *the sinner* became the *servant of God* (Job 42:7-7). Four times in these verses God called Job by that special Old Testament title "My servant". How did Job serve God? By enduring suffering and not cursing God, and thereby silencing the devil! Suffering in the will of God is a ministry that God gives to a chosen few." ____**Wiersbe**

God Denounces Job's Friends

God denounces Job's three friends in Job 42:7-8 for their arrogant false wisdom which had tormented Job and said, *"And so it was, after the Lord had spoken these words to Job, that the Lord said to Eliphaz the Temanite, My wrath is aroused against you and your two friends, for you have not spoken of Me what is right, as My servant Job has. Now therefore, take for yourselves seven bulls and seven rams, go to My servant Job, and offer up for yourselves a burnt offering; and My servant Job shall pray for you. For I will accept him, lest I deal with you according to your folly; because you have not spoken of Me what is right, as My servant Job has."*

A Storybook Ending

Job's three friends did as the Lord commanded them. And the Lord restored Job's losses when he prayed for his friends. In fact, the Lord gave Job twice as much as he had before. All his brothers and his sisters, and all those who had been his acquaintances before, came to him and ate food with him in his house; they consoled him and comforted him for all the adversity that the Lord had brought upon him. Each one gave him a piece of silver and each a ring of gold. The Scripture says the Lord blessed the last days of Job more than his beginning. He lived one hundred and forty years, and saw his children and grandchildren for four generations. So Job died, old and full of days.

Note: Job proves faithful to God in prosperity and in adversity. This surely is a model for us.

★ ★ ★

> "We buy things we don't need with money we don't have to impress people we don't like."
>
> – **Dave Ramsey**

> "Comfort and prosperity have never enriched the world as much as adversity has."
>
> – **Billy Graham**

"It's what you sow that multiplies, not what you keep in the barn."

– **Adrian Rogers**

"He is no fool who gives up what he cannot keep, to gain what he cannot lose."

– **Jim Elliot**, missionary

Questions for Personal Evaluation or Group Discussion

Chapter 9

1. Why would you want to seek financial wealth above and beyond your needs when you are already physically healthy, mentally stable and joyously happy, while caring for others?

2. Read Philippians 4:10-19 to determine how rich you can be. Also consider reading the book of Job.

3. Study the "Prosperity" gospel and the "Poverty" gospel to better understand how Satan tries to destroy lives.

4. Is God practical?

5. Explain Unconditional Love.

Notes

CHAPTER

X

"T-I-M-E"

Time Is My Eternity

"And do this, knowing the time, that now it is high time to awake out of sleep; for now our salvation is nearer than when we first believed."

– Romans 13:11

Definition of Time by Merriam-Webster … *the measured or measurable period during which an action, process, or condition exists or continues.* b. *a moment, second, minute, hour, day, or year as indicated by a clock or calendar*

We all know that time heals, steals and flies. Time is something we can't save, borrow, loan, store, buy, sell, hide, pause, trade, manufacture, or see. In essence, time is what it is, and time marches on silently. Time is like the wind, you can feel it coming, you can't see it leaving, but there is evidence it passed us by. While you can't see it, feel it or hear it, it's always been and will always continue with us.

The Nashville icon – Tennessee Williams said, "Time is the longest distance between two places."

It's been said, One of the greatest ways to commit murder, is to kill time.

Benjamin E. Mays said, *"I've only a minute, only sixty seconds in it. Forced upon me, can't refuse it, didn't seek it, didn't choose it, but it is up to me to use it. I must suffer if I lose it, give an account if I abuse it, just a tiny little minute, but eternity is in it."*

Time is the most valuable commodity on earth. You could have the finest home, along with great wealth and all the amenities of life, but by wasting time we squander the value of what using time wisely can produce.

This is why the Apostle Paul cautions us against the useless waste of time when he says in Ephesians 5:15-16, *"See then, that you walk circumspectly, not as fools, but as wise, redeeming the time, because the days are evil."*

Satan, our great adversary, wants us to waste time and in doing so destroy life, which God gives. Paul is cautioning Christians to use time wisely. The Greek word translated "redeeming" in this verse literally means to *buy up*. He is basically saying, "are you buying up each moment and using it in a productive manner?" Wasted time is irretrievable, it can't be bought back. Time is of more value than money. You can recover money that is wasted, not time.

The first commandment requires that we put God first or above all else (Exodus 20:2-3). We do what we want to do and go where we want to go. It's a matter of prioritizing and placing importance on what we find to be a priority. Jesus said, *"For where your treasure is, there your heart will be also."* God did not mean for us to set aside one single minute, hour or day of our lives for idleness, harmful deeds, or to waste time in doing nothing at all. We should determine to use our time to do good deeds in helping and benefiting our fellow man.

Often times, we mourn over the loss of something silly or meaningless, while having no regrets at all when we waste the most precious minutes of our allotted time.

Wikipedia offers this definition_____ *a dimension in which events can be ordered from the past through the present into the future, and also the measure of durations of events and the intervals between them.*

A few suggestions of time being wasted are: Complaining __Whining is really wasting time.

Procrastinating __Action always beats inaction.

Misuse of TV and Social Media, along with that of wasted time on video games and anything that just causes noise instead of wisely using quiet time.

Spending time with negative people __this can get to be contagious.

Looking for things misplaced __ practice keeping things in an orderly fashion.

Talking about unimportant things__ seek to communicate with substance.

Unnecessary use of the phone__ spending time in the Word of God and encouraging others.

Surfing the web endlessly __ allow technology to help you become a student of the Bible, as well as writing notes of encouragement to shut-ins.

Various Aspects of Time

The **past** relates to history. The **present** relates to now. The **future** is the indefinite time period after the present moment. Most of what we delay or propose to do in the future, we many times fail to complete, finish or even begin. While some people may see the future as predetermined, most see it as essentially unknown.

Time is used to discuss ageing, calendar of events, literature, setting time to music, differences in historical events, time out in sports, time changes across the world in various time zones, eternity and immortality, time in different cultures, philosophy, physics, psychology, chronological order, time management, perception, and even designating time to pray and study God's Word.

Valuing Time

As Christian parents and grandparents we should set aside or designate an allotted amount of time to train our children in the biblical ways of God, as well as attempting to meet their physical, social and materialistic needs in life. This is where we should seek balance or else this loss of time cannot be retracted.

Churches fail to grow properly as New Testament teaching offers us a pattern to exemplify. It is not enough to introduce people to Christ, but we need to follow up by seeing that they are discipled in the Gospel of Christ.

Don't ever think you don't have time for things that are necessary. There are 525,600 minutes in a year. Most time is wasted not in hours, but in minutes. A bucket of water with a hole in the bottom will become empty just like a bucket that is intentionally kicked over. We have wasted time in an airport waiting on a plane, only to realize I could have used that time wisely by initiating a conversation with someone in a positive manner. We often pray that God will grant us more quality time to use for Him and then misuse or lesson the quality of time God makes available to us. We all are given the same amount of time – 24 hours a day. It is how we choose to use it.

Time Management

A good example of time management in the Bible really begins with Moses when God had delivered him out of the hand of Pharaoh and the Egyptians. We see in Exodus 18:13-22, that Moses' father-in-law, Jethro, viewed the whole situation and noticed when Moses sat down to judge the people, that he tried to shoulder the whole load of offering counsel. Jethro told Moses to look out for able men throughout all the people and choose men who feared God and who were trustworthy and were honest to be placed over the people of the land. In verses 24-26, Moses listened to the voice of Jethro and shared and delegated qualified men to be heads over the people of Israel, chiefs of hundreds, of fifties, and of tens. And they judged the people at all times. Any hard case they brought to Moses, but any small matter, these men decided themselves. You might think Moses was a fast learner, while taking this class in "Time Management" at Jethro University.

Procrastination

Procrastination is defined as the action of delaying or postponing something. Procrastination is the avoidance of doing a task that needs to be accomplished. It is the practice of doing more pleasurable things in place of less pleasurable ones, or carrying out less urgent tasks to a later time. This occasionally creates problems in that …Why Wait? …till it's too late!

Although the word itself is not found in the Bible, there are many Scripture verses that imply the same principles. In Proverbs 13:4 we read, *"The soul of a lazy man desires, and has nothing; but the soul of the diligent shall be made rich."* Jesus illustrated the importance of being prepared for His coming in Matthew 25:1-13, when He spoke of the ten virgins who awaited the arrival of the bridegroom and the wedding feast. Five were prepared for His arrival; five failed to prepare until it was too late, and they were left behind. Jesus refers to the unprepared as being "foolish"; they were unprepared perhaps due to procrastination. For example, we should not ever have any reason to procrastinate in regards to eternal effects. Jesus could return at any time according to Luke 12:40, *"Therefore you also be ready, for the Son of Man is coming at an hour you do not expect."* Neither should we procrastinate or delay in dealing with anger against a brother.

The Time is Short

The Christian church has always been at its best in times when it was under extreme pressure. Over the past several years there has been a subtle and somewhat anemic approach to the presentation of the Gospel of Truth within a lot of local churches. A.W. Tozer is quoted as saying, *"Christianity has been watered down until the solution is so weak that if it were poison it would not hurt anyone, and if it were medicine it would not cure anyone!"* The Church in many areas has been weakened by apostasy, worldliness, compromise and apathy, that it appears to be in retreat rather than looking like the "Army of the Lord." The spirit of the Anti-Christ is sweeping the world.

Just as in the days when Christ was on this earth and He was training His Apostles, He is calling for unprecedented commitment. We don't need clock watchers in our churches; we need more preaching of the Gospel of Jesus Christ. We don't need more programs, but we need to disciple new converts every day with the pure and undefiled Word of God. Today is the day for action. The time has passed for indecision. The Church must rally its forces. Christians must consecrate themselves anew to Christ. We need to resolve that He alone is our Lord and we will serve Him only.

Many churches have become worldly and slothful; parents are not teaching their children in the homes, by wasting time on foolishness. The children are not being made aware of the Bible. We need to live close to God, so the children of following generations will rise up and call their parents blessed, because Almighty power will protect, infinite wisdom will guide and unchangeable goodness will prosper us.

Time is a Valuable Commodity

No one seems to have enough time, yet everyone has all the time there is. It is easy to be busy, while actually not accomplishing something. We all know how tricky the nature of time is, by staying busy and confusing activity with accomplishment. Time is a resource.

You can't buy it, rent it, borrow it, store it, renew it, or multiply it. All we can do is spend it. There is no way to "save" time. We can't save time for future use, because all time must be spent now. The rich can't buy more time and scientists can't invent more time. No one else can spend our time, just us. We sometimes refer to our health as being important to us, but become too busy to take time on exercising and eating healthy. What we do with our time determines where we place our values. All we have to decide is what to do with the time that is given to us. According to the Bible there is a Time for everything.

Ecclesiastes 3:1-8, *"To everything there is a season, a time for every purpose under heaven; a time to be born, and a time to die; a time to plant, and a time to pluck what is planted; a time to kill, and a time to heal; a time to break down, and a time to build up; a time to weep, and a time to laugh; a time to mourn, and a time to dance; a time to cast away stones, and a time to gather stones; a time to embrace, and a time to refrain from embracing; a time to gain, and a time to lose; a time to keep, and a time to throw away; a time to tear, and a time to sew; a time to keep silence, and a time to speak; a time to love, and a time to hate; a time of war, and a time of peace."*

★★★

Jesus said, *"I am the Way, the Truth and the Life"* -- If you love life, don't waste time, for time is what life is made up of in a measurable period, while Jesus is Eternal Life which cannot be measured.

★★★

"Lost time is never found Again."

Questions for Personal Evaluation or Group Discussion

Chapter 10

1. How valuable is time and is there a price that can be placed on time?

2. Explain what the Apostle Paul meant in Ephesians 5:15-16, concerning the passage, "redeeming the time."

3. Discuss 'Time Management' verses 'Procrastination'.

4. Time is a valuable commodity. How does Ecclesiastes 3:1-8, depict or characterize the various uses of our allotted time?

Notes

CHAPTER

"Problems We Manufacture"

"We cannot solve our problems with the same thinking we used when we created them."

– Albert Einstein

Human Frailties and Fallibilities

These two words are common in all our lives and have been since the fall in the garden. Only God is infallible. Therefore, this is why God sent His only Begotten Son, Jesus, to guide and offer direction through His example. Always remember, Jesus is the Way, the Truth and the Life.

In this chapter we will look at how we can eliminate and incorporate those items which would tend to help our lifestyles. All throughout this book we all must reiterate that we are sinners and need a Savior. Satan is walking to and fro seeking whom he may devour.

People are seeking answers, but many times in all the wrong places. God does not reveal himself through the Psychic Circle, such as astrology, palmistry, fortune telling, Ouija boards, Tarot cards, crystal balls and various mediums or forms of divination (which is covered later in this chapter), but ONLY through His Word, which is Jesus, God's only begotten Son.

Homosexuality

With the help of many main-line churches, politicians, educators and judges, the so-called "Gay Rights Movement" has been successful in promoting homosexuality as an acceptable part of society. When Scripture and culture appear to disagree, we must stand with God's Word. Homosexual behavior is clearly condemned in the Bible. *"You shall not lie with a male as with a woman. It is an abomination" (Leviticus 18:22).* We also read in 1 Corinthians 6:9-11, *"Do you not know that the unrighteous will not inherit the kingdom of God? Do not be deceived. Neither fornicators, nor idolaters, nor adulterers, nor homosexuals, nor sodomites, nor thieves, nor covetous, nor drunkards, nor revilers, nor extortioners will inherit the kingdom of God. And such were some of you. But you were washed, but you were sanctified, but you were justified in the name of the Lord Jesus and by the Spirit of our God."*

The word "abomination" is defined in the noun form as ___ atrocity, disgrace, obscenity, evil, monstrosity and a thing that causes disgust or hatred. If God would have approved of the homosexual lifestyle, He would not have referred to it as an abomination. As with all sins, the root problem is idolatry; substituting man-made gods in place of the one, true God of the Bible. Romans 1:18-32 addresses the sin of homosexuality most fully. As far back in the early Old Testament days, God warned His people against such sexual action, along with other aspects of paganism.

The term **LGBT**, that stands for lesbian, gay, bisexual, and transgender, has been in use since the 1990s. Prior to the 1950s, **homosexual** was used, at which was replaced with the term **homophile** in the 1950s and 1960s, and subsequently the term **gay** in the 1970s

Man's Choice

God created man in His image and likeness, then took a rib out of man and formed woman and formed the first marriage. He then told them to replenish the earth.

Many in today's world believe they were created as homosexuals, but that is far from the truth, rather it is a Choice. Seemingly, the best article ever written to explain in detail the subject of Homosexuality is entitled ________

"10 Things Everyone Should Know About a Christian View of Homosexuality" (2014)

Copied with permission by Glenn Stanton, associated with Focus on the Family.

1. All humans are simultaneously sinful and loved. All people, regardless of their story, are deeply and unconditionally loved by God, each created with profound dignity and worth, not one more than another. This is more than religious "Happy Talk" – its truth whether one is gay, straight, or otherwise. But, all people are also stricken with a terminal illness: SIN. Everyone. No exceptions and to the same degree. Our sin demands our repentance and needs forgiveness, and God's love and grace are where we find both. This is basic Christianity and the great equalizer of all people.

2. Jesus wasn't silent on homosexuality. Some claim Jesus never said anything about homosexuality and therefore is neutral on the topic. Not true. Jesus was unequivocal in saying that to understand marriage and the sexual union, we must go back to the beginning and see how God created humanity and to what end (See Matthew 19 and Mark 10). Jesus holds up the creation story in Genesis not as a quaint Sunday school lesson, but as authoritative --- reminding us that God created each of us male and female, each for the other. And the sexual union that God created and ordains is for husband and wife to come together in physical union, one flesh.

3. There is only one option. Both Jesus and all of Scripture approve of no other sexual union than that between a husband and wife. This is the uncontested historical teaching of Judaism and Christianity, and it is not something that true Christianity is free to adjust with the times. Yes, concubines and multiple wives are found in the Bible, but it doesn't make them "biblical". In fact, they violate the Genesis narrative Christ points us to.

4. Male and female complete God's image on earth. It is not just mere "traditionalism" that makes sex-distinct marriage the norm for Christians. It is a common grace God has given to all peoples at all times that is rooted in deeper theological reasons. The first chapter of the Jewish and Christian scriptures tells us that humanity is uniquely created to show forth the image of God in the world – to make visible the invisible. God does this not just in generic, androgynous humanity, but through two very similar but distinct types of humans: male and female. They are human universals, not cultural constructs.

When God said that it "is not good that the man be alone" (Genesis 2:18) he wasn't lamenting that Adam didn't have a buddy or was just lonely. He was saying that the male could not really know himself as male without a human "other" who equally shared his humanity but was meaningfully distinct right down to every bit of her DNA. The same is true for her in Adam. In both Jewish and Christian belief, both male and female become fully human in their correspondence and contrast with one another. This does not happen solely in marriage, but it does happen most profoundly and mysteriously in marriage.

5. Sex is indeed about babies. It is a new and culturally peculiar idea that human sexuality is all about intimacy and pleasure, but not necessarily babies. Babies and reproduction matter. And sure, while not every male/female sexual engagement is toward the end of procreation – intimacy and pleasure matter as well – it has been the overwhelming norm and desire in nearly all marital relationships throughout time. That some couples are infertile either by age or incapability does not diminish or challenge this reality. Infertility is the vast exception for male/female couples. It is the fact of same-sex unions, a human cul-de-sac. Heterosexual union reaches into and creates the next generation. To establish a sexual relationship without any interest in or openness to babies is contrary to God's intention for such relationships.

6. Children have a right to a mother and father. Every person ever born can track his origin to a mother and a father. There are no exceptions, including those artificially produced. This was the first command God gave to the first two humans: to come together and bring forth the coming generations of new divine image-bearers. Nearly all cultures in all places in the world at all historical times hold as fundamental that every child should be loved and raised by mother and father.

7. Same-sex attraction is not sin. To be human is to have a disordered sexuality. You do, I do. Everyone does. We all have some manner of sexual drive that compels us to disobey God's design for sexuality. But while temptation is universal, it's different from sin. Scripture tells us that Jesus was tempted in all ways as we are, but did not sin (see Hebrews 4:15). Sexual sin is giving in to that desire in either mind or body. Faithful Christian discipleship cannot avoid temptation, but it strives to resist and master it along with God's help through obedience and dependence upon Christ.

Many are indeed same-sex attracted, but live obediently within a Christian sexual ethic. It can be difficult, as it is for heterosexuals who are required to live in celibacy. Christianity requires that we each bring our sexual (and many other) desires to our faith commitment – and countless same-sex attracted believers do so willingly and joyfully.

8. Sexual intimacy is not a right. Every Christian has limitations placed on his sexuality. For married Christians, it is exclusive to one's spouse. For single, engaged, and divorced Christians, it is abstinence, no exceptions. It is unfair for so many to be forced into a life that cannot know the wonder and beauty of physical intimacy just because marriage is not an option for them? Is it fair for a Christian to be stuck in a loveless marriage? Christians have long understood that fairness is not really the question. Sex is not a right, but a gift --- and the giver knows what is best for us.

9. Rewriting God's rules is never an option. One of the marks of a Christian is his or her desire to be obedient to Christ's teaching. Certainly most of us would like to rewrite the scriptures to make life easier. However, Christianity is a demanding faith. The scriptures define and change us, not the other way around. A biblical sexual ethic does not, and cannot, change with the times.

10. People are more than their sexuality. As we grow in Jesus Christ, who is the Word, we begin to mature as a servant of Christ and better understand the words of the Apostle Paul when he says in 1 Thessalonians 4:3-8 *"For this is the will of God, your sanctification: that you should abstain from sexual immorality; ..."*

Sexual Immorality

What is sexual immorality? The connection between sexual immorality and idolatry is best understood in 1 Corinthians 6:18, which says, *"Flee from sexual immorality."* Verse 19 says the bodies of believers are the "temple of the Holy Spirit". Pagan idol worship often saw perverse and immoral sexual acts performed in the temple of a false god. In other words, when we use our physical bodies for immoral purposes, we are imitating pagan worship by profaning God's holy temple with acts He calls detestable. A word often translated "sexual immorality" is *porneia*. From this Greek word we get the English word *pornography*.

Since sexuality is God's design, only God can define the parameters for its use. In Genesis the Bible is clear that sex was created to be enjoyed between one man and one woman who are in a covenant marriage until one of them dies (Matthew 19:6). Anything other than this is outside God's design.

God Never Changes

Many people, especially those who fail to read and study the Bible, God's infallible Word, tend to think times have changed from that of biblical times and what was once sin is no longer considered sin (Read Galatians 5:19-25).

We read in Hebrews 13:8 *"Jesus Christ is the same yesterday, today, and forever."*

"For I am the Lord, I do not change" (Malachi 3:6).

We fool ourselves when we think that we can stubbornly choose sin and God does not care. 1 John 2:3-4 says, *"Now by this we know that we know Him, if we keep His commandments. He who says, 'I know Him,' and does not keep His commandments, is a liar, and the truth is not in him."*

Words such as Adultery, which means a married person having sexual intercourse with someone other than their mate; Fornication, meaning those having sexual intercourse that are not married. These words are not very seldom used today.

Satan has changed his vocabulary, some of his methods of deceit, his neon signs, his media, and his looks, but he is still doing everything he can to destroy the faith of God's people. He is the accuser of the brethren, the tempter of mankind, a murderer, a counterfeiter, and as cunning as when the serpent beguiled Eve in the garden through his subtility. Paul said, *"But I fear, lest somehow, as the serpent deceived Eve by his craftiness, so your minds may be corrupted from the simplicity that is in Christ" (2 Corinthians 11:3-4).* Paul also said in verses 13-15, *"For such are false apostles, deceitful workers, transforming themselves into apostles of Christ. And no wonder! For Satan himself transforms himself into an angel of light. Therefore it is no great thing if his ministers also transform themselves into ministers of righteousness, whose end will be according to their works."*

Satan is known as the great deceiver, in that he offers a counterfeit spirit, a counterfeit Jesus and a counterfeit gospel.

An Occult Check List to Consider

Divination, an occult practice is forbidden in Deuteronomy 18:9-14 and the practice is of a forbidden psychic origin. While it is not biblical to become legalistic in our preaching and teaching, it is important to warn against the occult and pagan sins of divination. If you should read Acts 19:17-19, *"This became known both to all Jews and Greeks dwelling in Ephesus; and fear fell on them all, and the name of the Lord Jesus was magnified. And many who had believed came confessing and telling their deeds. Also, many of those who had practiced magic brought their books together and burned them in the sight of all. And they counted up the value of them, and it totaled fifty thousand pieces of silver."*

Not many people today are aware of those things in the following occult check list: **Animism**: the belief that souls inhabit all or most objects. **Astrology**: consulting the zodiac or star signs. **Buddhism**: worship & study Gautama the enlightened. **Charming**: (as in casting spells, hypnotism). **Crystal Ball**: divination, a means of prediction, foretelling. **Death magic**: spells placed in coffin or grave. **Drugs**: (psychotropic producing hallucinogenic effects, e.g. Acid, Ice, marijuana, coke, speed, heroin, LSD, etc). **Dungeons & Dragons**; **WarCraft**; **Diabalo** and other fantasy role-play games involving occult & violent themes. **Eastern Mysticism**: including Yoga, TM, and Mantras. **Exorcism**: an occultic attempt to evict demonic spirits. **Fortune telling**: palmistry, tea leaf reading, etc. **Freemasonry**: the Lodge, Illuminati, and secret societies. **Handwriting analysis**: for occult prediction. **Hexes**: invoked against a real or perceived enemy. **Horoscopes**: daily, weekly, yearly prognostications. **Hypnosis, hypnotism**: using post hypnotic trance states. **Idols**: Buddha, Kali, Totems, statues of Mary, etc. **Levitation**: lifting objects using unseen spiritual forces. **Magic**: (not sleight of hand) but supernatural. **Mediums**: psychics & channellers linking the spirit world. **Mental telepathy**: psychic mental communications. **Mind Control**: both overt and covert. **Mysticism**: and attempt to find God through asceticism. **Necromancy**: calling up spirits impersonating the dead. **Numerology**: using number combinations predicatively. **Ouija Boards**: the most dangerous of all occult devices. **Pagan rites**: Voodoo, sing sings, fire walking, or on broken glass, body piercing, shamanism, bloodletting, umbanda, macumba, Santeria, etc. **Parakineses**: moving objects by mind and will power. **Sorcery**: Use of black arts through witches or warlocks. **Superstition**: fear based beliefs, often from family lore. **Tattoos, body piercing, self mutilation** (Leviticus 19:28). Transcendal Meditation: sanitized Hinduism. **Urology/ uropathy**: practice of drinking one's own urine.

Anyone who identifies with the area of involvement mentioned above, should forsake such and realize these were practices that God spoke against in referring to the occult and ancient pagan sins of divination and should not be a part of today's culture.

Foundations and Consequences

Psalm 11:3 says, "If the foundations are destroyed, what can the righteous do?"

Think about it: Nobody – no politician, economist, or financial expert can explain why great institutions are failing. Why our school systems are failing, our government is failing. The Lord is laying bare all the foundations that men have trusted for a long time. But the one thing that cannot be shaken by God's judgment is the church of the Lord Jesus Christ.

Let's just look back over the past fifty years and notice some drastic changes that have taken place or need to be changed. (1) Our local churches (as a whole) have been watering down the gospel preaching of the Cross, Sin, Hell, the Judgment Seat of Christ, Sanctification, the Book of Revelation, the purity of the heart, and discipleship. Churches should be preaching the infallible Word of God, instead of being entertainment centers. The House of God, rather than contemporary music halls and afraid to teach biblical doctrine for fear of not maintaining the attendance and loosing financial support.

Looking for new programs that offer little or no substance in the Word. (2) Christian homes with a mother and a father to raise the children to know and love God. (3) Schools for the primary purpose of educating our children rather than sharing their political viewpoints and misusing the tax money intended for developing reading, writing, grammar and communication skills in order for our students to become strong in a weak world.

A Look at Our Secular Nation

The greatest majority of our modern society thinks only about money or monetary value.

The majority of our world thinks one of two things in regards to dying. (1) Everyone goes to Heaven or (2) there is no Heaven or Hell.

Sports have become gods to a great number in today's world (especially on Sunday).

So-called sports heroes make up a large percentage of our violent crimes and fail to exemplify normal outstanding characteristics in a good common society.

The eating of food, as well as gluttony have become gods to many. Food should be for nourishment and stability.

We don't need Gun Control, but rather Self-Control. No gun has ever had to be counseled or walked out of a house by itself and shot anyone.

Men and women need to realize the only place Success comes before Work is in Webster's Dictionary.

Our judicial system is corrupt and should be reconstructed to become uniformly standardized across our United States.

Call No man Reverend __ (Psalm 111:9) "...holy and reverend is His name." KJV

Our government officials in local, state and national levels (especially members of congress) should be good examples through their speech, character, so as to better influence our children, at least while they are serving in office. Many of them exemplify such low character and self-esteem it becomes an embarrassment to all.

Our prisons and jails should be advertized as such. No televisions, exercise equipment, basketball courts, libraries and allowances for good behavior. They should have to work six to eight hours five days a week on the Chain Gang, eating basic food and water. Nothing but isolation and a cot in their cells. Note: This information should be published in our newspapers and taught in our schools, so that no one would ever want to go there.

Two weeks after graduating from high school all males and females, including most handicaps, should have to serve two years in the military (handicaps doing some type of office work or other regimented services). Then after that two year period, they could enlist or attend Officer Training School, if they so desired.

Some things that need to be eliminated in today's world are the following – Hollywood, eighty percent of TV shows, gambling casinos and lotteries, beer gardens and bars (since people coming out of these have a high level of alcohol in their system) get into cars and travel on our highways. Pornography and human trafficking has become a major hazard.

Bitter water and sweet water doesn't flow out of the same stream. Therefore, blessing and cursing should not come out of the same mouth. Trash mouths are sewer mouths. We must not confuse the term "Wordy Dirds or Dirty Words" as being part of the English language.

A simple way to define "Retirement" is you work one day and get tired and you work the next day and re-tire. Therefore, to properly retire one should never stop working, at least if it's something enjoyable that keeps one's mind active.

To best summarize all of the above: In contrast to a world that increasingly presents reality in a distorted, inaccurate and deceptive means, the truth and summation of all human reality is given by the Word of our Lord and Savior with the endpoint being Heaven or Hell.

* * *

> *"God did not make us robots. In spite of the denial by Luther, Calvin, and many evangelical leaders today, God gave man a will to freely choose to love or to hate Him, to receive Christ as Savior and Lord or to reject Him."*
>
> **– Dave Hunt**

Why Problems Occur

When we look back in the Old Testament at the account of the shepherd boy, David, we see he was delivering lunch to his brothers, according to the instructions of his father, Jesse. They, along with King Saul, were in the Valley of Elah, doing battle against the Philistines. As you read the full account in 1 Samuel 17, you will notice that the young boy David was ashamed that the armies of Israel would fear and tremble before the giant, Goliath. Without hesitation he presented himself to King Saul and stepped up against Goliath without even considering the size of the giant. It was with complete confidence in the God who had proven Himself to be faithful to David in past times.

When we fail to place our confidence fully in the God of the Bible, we should be afraid. From a child, David had learned to trust God, while as a boy keeping his father's sheep. As a result, God allowed one of five small smooth stones to travel from young David's sling shot and find its mark in the forehead of Goliath's most vulnerable exposed part of his armor. This is a good example of how when we seek to do things our way and amidst our thinking, we fail simply because God who is all knowing, desires us to seek Him and His direction in our lives.

"Never worry about tomorrow, but enjoy today and trust God for another today in a better way."

Lack of Concentration

Whether we are working off a ladder or driving a vehicle, we should keep our mind on our present activity which we are engaged in. Taking our eyes off the road just for a second could cause a wreck. On a much larger scale, until we notice the importance of Salvation through Christ Jesus, we are as Paul mentions in 1 Corinthians 15:19, *"If in this life only we have hope in Christ, we are of all men most pitiable."*

We are prone to make poor choices when we fail to concentrate on the important issues of life. For example, taking care of necessities first, not spending in excess of your income, failing to plan is planning to fail, and time management.

There's an old saying, "Only one life will soon be past, only what's done for Christ will last." Since it is inevitable we all must die, the old Boy Scout Motto "BE PREPARED" comes into play.

The Keys to the Kingdom

Keys are used to lock or unlock doors. The specific doors Jesus has in mind in this passage of Scripture are the doors to the Kingdom of Heaven. It is important to understand how, biblically speaking, one enters the Kingdom of Heaven. Jesus said, unless one is "Born Again", he will not see the Kingdom of Heaven (John 3:3). One is born again when the Holy Spirit works through the Word of God (Jesus) to bring about new life in a dead sinner. As you read Romans 10:8-13, you will notice the faithful preaching of the gospel is the key to the Kingdom.

In Matthew 16:19, Jesus is specifically addressing Peter, so in the Book of Acts, Peter fits prominently in 'opening doors' to three different groups of people so they can enter the Kingdom. (1) In Acts 2, Peter preaches in Jerusalem on the Day of Pentecost, about three thousand Jewish people were saved that day. (2) Later, in Acts 8, the Samaritans believe the gospel and receive the Holy Spirit. Here, Peter unlocked the door for the Samaritans. (3) Then in Acts 10, Peter unlocked the door for the Gentiles.

Also, keys can be used to lock doors, as well as open them. For instance, the Bible says, in Genesis 6:5, *"the Lord saw that the wickedness of man was great in the earth, and that every "intent" of the thoughts of his heart was only evil continually."* But Noah obeyed and walked with God.

Verse 8 says, *"But Noah found grace in the eyes of the Lord."* And God told Noah to build an Ark in verse 14, and the flood came. In chapter 7, He had Noah, his family and the animals God instructed him to take on the Ark to enter it after which time God shut the door of the Ark. Noah did all that God had instructed him to do, which was the key of obedience. It's only wise to remember – "What God closes, no man can open and what God opens, no man can close."

The greatest problem in the world is the problem of not having God, who is the greatest problem solver. He who made us is able to keep us and love us with the greatest love, because God is Love. Like the song writer, Carolyn Gillman, who in her classic song – "And He's Ever Interceding", we can be greatly elated when reading *Hebrews 7:22-28*.

The above passage of Scripture is no doubt one of the most profound statements of proclamation in the entire world. No king, prince, president, or person of royalty; no artifact or literary work and not even the best of brains can conceive a higher plateau of thinking.

"Either God is Lord over all or He is not God at all."

* * *

Highly recommended for Wall-Mounting

"Jesus, High Priest Forever"

"By so much more Jesus has become a surety of a better covenant. Also there were many priests, because they were prevented by death from continuing. But He, because He continues forever, has an unchangeable priesthood. Therefore He is also able to save to the uttermost those who come to God through Him, since He always lives to make intercession for them. For such a High Priest was fitting for us, who is holy, harmless, undefiled, separate from sinners, and has become higher than the heavens; who does not need daily, as those high priests, to offer up sacrifices, first for His own sins and then for the people's, for this He did once for all when He offered up himself. For the law appoints as high priests men who have weakness, but the word of the oath, which came after the law, appoints the Son who has been perfected forever" (Hebrews 7:26-28).

"He Paid it all On Calvary"

Questions for Personal Evaluation or Group Discussion

Chapter 11

1. What are some examples where people tend to look for answers in wrong places?

2. Notice the sharp contrast of the occult practice of Divination, forbidden in Deuteronomy 18:9-14 in the Old Testament, verses what happened through the preaching of Paul in Acts 19:11-20 in the New Testament.

3. Should we as Christians forsake the practices that God spoke against in referring to the occult and ancient pagan sins of Divination and not be a part of today's culture?

4. Discuss the Keys to the Kingdom.

Notes

CHAPTER

"Making Good Choices"

"You are your choices"

All throughout life it is our choices that reveal who we are, far more than our abilities. We may make many choices in our time span, but there is one which God will not forgive us – the rejection of His Son, Jesus Christ.

What Does the Bible Say?

"There is a way that seems right to a man, but its end is the way of death" (Proverbs 14:12). We all have thoughts and ambitions of what we want to become in life, however, as a Christian the Bible encourages us to *"Trust in the Lord with all your heart, and lean not on your own understanding" (Proverbs 3:5-6).*

Choices We All Need to Make

If you are reading this book and you have not surrendered your life to Jesus Christ, this is truly no coincidence, as much prayer has gone up in your behalf. You may say, "I'm a good person. I would never hurt anybody. I am honest. I love and care for my family. Surely I will go to Heaven when I die." While it may be true and most people are pretty good, contrary to popular opinion, not all good people go to Heaven. In fact, you do not have to be a bad person to go to hell. Notice what the Bible says in Titus 3:5: *"Not by works of righteousness which we have done, but according to His mercy He saved us..."* The Bible also states in Ephesians 2:8-9, *"For by grace are you saved through faith; and that not of yourselves: it is the gift of God: Not of works, lest any man should boast."*

Another interesting fact found in the Bible is that you are not really as good as you think you are. Ecclesiastes 7:20 states, *"For there is not a just man upon earth, that doeth good, and sinneth not." "As it is written, There is none righteous, no, not one: for all have sinned, and come short of the glory of God" (Romans 3:10, 23).*

It is true that you must have goodness to get to Heaven, but the truth is you do not possess that goodness in and of yourself. *"But your iniquities have separated you from your God; and your sins have hidden His face from you, so that He will not hear" (Isaiah 59:2). "For the wages of sin is death; but the gift of God is eternal life through Jesus Christ our Lord" (Romans 6:23).* In reality, everyone deserves to die and go to hell because of their sin; however, Jesus loved us so much that He shed His sinless blood and died in our place. Three days later, Christ rose from the grave, proving that He had conquered death and hell, and establishing that He alone has the power to give us eternal life. *"But God commended His love toward us, in that, while we were yet sinners, Christ died for us" (Romans 5:8).*

Dwell on this. If our goodness could save us, Jesus would have died in vain. The fact is no one can possibly get to Heaven on his own. Jesus stated in John 14:6, *"I am the way, the truth, and the life: no man cometh unto the Father, but by me."*

You say, how can I receive Christ into my life? It is very simple. First, you must be genuinely sorry for your sin. Luke 13:3 states, *"... unless you repent, you will all likewise perish."* True repentance produces a new way of living.

Secondly, you must believe that Jesus died for you. *"That if you confess with your mouth the Lord Jesus and believe in your heart that God has raised Him from the dead, you will be saved. For with the heart man believeth unto righteousness; and with the mouth confession is made unto salvation" (Romans 10:9-10).*

Finally, ask Him to save you and take you to Heaven when you die. *"For whosoever shall call upon the name of the Lord shall be saved" (Romans 10:13).* What a tragedy it would be for a good person or anyone to die and go to hell.

Do you realize that there will be "religious" people that will go to hell? That meaning: there are those who attend church regularly, they may sing in the choir, preach, hold positions in the church and even quote set prayers; but because they have never sincerely confessed their sin, asked Jesus into their heart, or called upon His name, and by faith received Him into their heart, they will be eternally lost and go to hell. Always remember God's Word, the Bible, is our *Basic Instructions Before Leaving Earth.*

Choose Forgiveness

In the Bible, the Greek word that is translated "forgiveness" literally means "to let go," as instead of holding a grudge against someone or demanding a payment for a debt. Jesus said in Luke 11:4 *"And forgive us our sins, for we also forgive everyone who is indebted to us. And do not lead us into temptation, but deliver us from the evil one."* When you forgive, you are not disregarding that which is wrong or acting as if it never happened; you are simply letting it go.

None of us are perfect. James 3:2 says, *"For we all stumble in many things. If anyone does not stumble in word, he is a perfect man, able to bridle the whole body."*

Plan to forgive and make reconciliation as soon as possible, rather than letting your anger fester. Ephesians 4:26, 27 *"Be angry, and do not sin: do not let the sun go down on your wrath."*

Choose to Love God and Others

The more we love God, the more love we can bestow on our family and others. Always remember to put God first and foremost. God not only has love – God is love (1John 4:8). Love is what prompted Christ's saving efforts on the Cross (John 3:16). Isaiah lets us know that God's love is even greater than that of a nursing mother. Isaiah 49:15 *"Can a woman forget her nursing child, and not have compassion on the son of her womb? Surely they may forget, yet I will not forget you."* And we read in John 13:35, *"By this all will know that you are My disciples, if you have love for one another."*

Choose to Serve God

> *"I long for nothing more earnestly than to serve God with all my heart."*
>
> – Charles Spurgeon

Jesus said, "And you shall love the Lord your God with all your heart, with all your soul, with all your mind, and with all your strength. This is the first commandment. And the second, like it, is this: You shall love your neighbor as yourself. There is no other commandment greater than these" (Mark 12:29-31). You may retire from a career, but never from the work and service of God. Once we are enlisted in the army of God, we see He is working out a plan in our lives that keeps us forever employed in His Kingdom work.

Choose to Meditate on Good Things

This is not to be taken out of context of scripture, such as in Transcendental Meditation or in Yoga, rather in reference to Philippians 4:8-9, *"Finally, brethren, whatever things are true, whatever things are noble, whatever things are just, whatever things are pure, whatever things are lovely, whatever things are of good report, if there is any virtue and if there is anything praiseworthy – meditate on these things. The things which you learned and received and heard and saw in me, these do, and the God of peace will be with you."*

Note: As mentioned earlier in the book, Satan is a liar and the father of all liars. Just to show how cunning Satan is --- there was a British philosophical writer named James Allen who lived from (1864-1912). He was considered a pioneer of the self-help movement. His best known work, "As a Man Thinketh", published in 1903, took the scripture which reads *"For as he thinks in his heart, so is he" (Proverbs 23:7)* out of context as further verified in 1 Corinthians 2:14, *"But the natural man does not receive the things of the Spirit of God, for they are foolishness to him; nor can he know them, because they are spiritually discerned."*

While James Allan is one of many (so called prolific writers in today's world), this is only one of many examples of how Satan is and has always been attempting to destroy the minds of mankind. Deception is a lie reduced to practice.

Satan is so deceptive that many of the pastors of what was known as Evangelical churches in the 1970s and 1980s are now allowing TM and Yoga classes to be taught during the mid-week hours of their church schedules.

Attention!!! Do Not Be Deceived. Be SURE.....to seek for a Solid BIBLE Teaching Church. Read and study your Bible every day and pour out your heart in prayer to God for the TRUTH of His Word. This is Your Choice. Do not Waste it. Make it count for all Eternity.

The Message that should be sounded from our churches today is found in Revelation 3:14-22. Verse 20 says, "Behold, I stand at the door and knock. If anyone hears My voice and opens the door, I will come in to him and dine with him, and he with Me."

Verse 22 says, "He who has an ear, let him hear what the Spirit says to the churches"

Choose Eternal Life

Your eternal destiny will not be the result of chance but of choice. Perhaps you are thinking you are young and have plenty of time. No one knows how much time we have on this earth. None of us know the hour or under what circumstances we will leave this life. God warned the people in the days of Noah. They failed to listen. God told Jonah to go to Nineveh, a very wicked city and warn its inhabitants that their city will be destroyed in 40 days. Jonah was afraid to go and took a boat across the Mediterranean in the opposite direction. However, God caused a great storm to come and Jonah was thrown overboard by the sailors on the ship. God prepared a great fish (perhaps a whale) to swallow Jonah, and later the fish spits him out onto dray land. Again, God commands Jonah to go to Nineveh and warn the people. This time Jonah obeys and the people respond. They repent, and the city is spared. Jonah was angry with God when the city is not destroyed, but God showed compassion on the people, as well as their cattle (Jonah 4:11).

Contrary to a lot of people's perception of the Old Testament God, Ezekiel quotes God as saying, *"As I live, says the Lord God, I have no pleasure in the death of the wicked, but that the wicked turn from his way and live. Turn, turn from your evil ways! For why should you die, O house of Israel?"(Ezekiel 33:11).*

The Bible warns that in the final days of earth's history evil will once again become rampant. In Revelation 16:18-20 it mentions an earthquake will be so terrible that the world's mountains will flatten and the islands of the sea will disappear. God is constantly warning the world of this terrible calamity. In Revelation 14:6-7, *"Then I saw another angel flying in the midst of heaven, having the everlasting gospel to preach to those who dwell on the earth – to every nation, tribe, tongue, and people – saying with a loud voice, "Fear God and give glory to Him, for the hour of His judgment has come; and worship Him who made heaven and earth, the sea and springs of water."*

The truth of the matter is this, we are all on a trip moving through this world, not knowing when or where we'll die, but we need to be aware this earth is not our final home. In the gospel of Matthew 7:13-14, we are told to *"enter by way of the narrow gate; for wide is the gate and broad is the way that leads to destruction, and there are many who go in by it. Because narrow is the gate and difficult is the way which leads to life, and there are few who find it."*

Jesus said in Luke 7:24, *"Therefore whoever hears these sayings of Mine, and does them, I will liken him to a wise man who built his house on the rock."*

Choose Thankfulness

This is basically possessing an attitude of gratitude. The Scriptures urge believers to maintain a spirit of thanksgiving in all situations and in all circumstances.

Giving thanks realigns our hearts with that of the Apostle Paul's expression of praise in his letters to the Romans: "For of Him and through Him and to Him are all things, to whom be glory forever. Amen" (Romans 11:36).

The lyrics of the old hymn – "Count your blessings, name them one by one. Count your many blessings, see what God has done"—this is a way of expressing our gratefulness. As God's children we should be constantly focused the words of Philippians 4:19, *"And my God shall supply all your need according to His riches in Glory by Christ Jesus."* And remember the words of Deuteronomy 31:6, *"Be strong and of good courage, do not fear nor be afraid of them; for the Lord your God, He is the One who goes with you. He will not leave you nor forsake you."*

Choose Joy Over Happiness

Happiness comes and goes. Happiness is for a moment, while the joy of the Lord is eternal and internal. Happiness is a circumstance, Joy is a choice. We often hear people say, "Happy Easter" or "Merry Christmas" or "Happy Birthday", etc. In a sense, happiness can be described as a result of circumstances. As a Christian, we should think about what this word, joy, means. Many times you see shirts different ones wear with messages of Joy and Peace. However, you wonder if they know what those words really mean.

How can you live by something if you don't know its meaning? Simply stated, joy is a result of choice. When we invite Christ into our lives His Joy creates a change as we grow in Him and we change by becoming more like Christ. Therefore, His joy will be ever present, even during difficult times. Joy comes in many forms. Sometimes it is found in worship and singing, sometimes in the quiet presence of the Lord, other times during sickness or to sustain you in the loss of a loved one. Happiness and sorrow are a part of our existence. Regardless of the emotion, God's joy is present.

Someone said, "Joy Comes in the Morning". John 15:11, *"These things I have spoken to you, that My joy may remain in you, and that your joy may be full."* What do "these things" mean? "These things" refer to what Jesus said prior to John 15:11, in verses 9-10 it says, *"As the Father loved me I also have loved you; abide in My love. If you keep My commandments, you will abide in My love, just as I have kept My Father's commandments and abide in His love."* Notice the sequence. Verse 9 – to have joy you have to abide in God's love; Verse 10 – to abide in God's love you have to obey God's commands.

Choose Obedience

Jesus Himself was obedient according to Philippians 2:8 *"And being found in appearance as a man, He humbled Himself and became obedient to the point of death, even the death of the cross."*

Obedience is defined as "dutiful or submissive compliance to the commands of one in authority." *"Submissive"* indicates that we yield our wills to God's. Our obedience to God is not solely a matter of duty. As we grow in obedience however, our obedience to God's commands will allow us to become both Light and Salt in a dark and tasteless world" (Matthew 5:13-16).

As we read in Matthew 26:36-39, *"Then Jesus came with them to a place called Gethsemane, and said to the disciples, "Sit here while I go and pray over there."And He took with Him Peter and the two sons of Zebedee, and He began to be sorrowful and deeply distressed. Then He said to them, 'My soul is exceedingly sorrowful, even to death, Stay here and watch with Me." He went a little farther and fell on His face, and prayed, saying, 'O My Father, if it is possible, let this cup pass from Me; nevertheless, not as I will, but as You will.'* Mark 32:37-42, *"Then He came and found them sleeping, and said to Peter, 'Simon, are you sleeping? Could you not watch one hour? Watch and pray, lest you enter into temptation. The spirit indeed is willing, but the flesh is weak.' Again He went away and prayed, and spoke the same words. And when He returned He found them asleep again, for their eyes were heavy; and they did not know what to answer Him. Then He came the third time and said to them, 'Are you still sleeping and resting? It is enough! The hour is come; behold, the Son of Man is being betrayed into the hands of sinners. Rise, let us be going. See, My betrayer is at hand."* It is here we look to Luke 22:43-44, as reference is being made while He was praying – *"Then an angel appeared to Him from Heaven, strengthening Him. And being in agony, He prayed more earnestly. Then His sweat became like great drops of blood falling down to the ground."*

NOTE: Prior to the crucifixion, as Jesus Christ prayed in the garden of Gethsemane, Luke, the physician, mentioned in the Gospel of Luke 22:44, *"And being in agony, He prayed more earnestly. Then His sweat became like great drops of blood falling down to the ground."*

This was written by the physician Luke, a well-educated man and a careful observer by profession. Luke is the only one of the synoptic gospels to mention the bloody sweat, probably because as a physician he perhaps noticed this rare physiological phenomenon of agony Jesus was suffering.

According to Dr. Frederick Zugibe, (Chief Medical Examiner of Rockland County, New York) "although this medical condition is relatively rare, it is well-known, and there have been many cases of it. The clinical term is "hematohidrosis". Dr. Zugibe goes on to say, "Around the sweat glands, there are multiple blood vessels in a net-like form." Under the pressure of great stress the vessels constrict. Then as the anxiety passes "the blood vessels dilate to the point of rupture. The blood goes into the sweat glands." As the sweat glands are producing a lot of sweat, it pushes the blood to the surface – coming out as droplets of blood mixed with sweat.

This is descriptive of the great stress and intense anguish Jesus suffered, as He was facing the most horrible capital punishment anyone could ever face. Remember, He had a human body, which could feel all the pain as we would. Above and beyond the physical stress, we cannot begin to understand the mental stress, as He was about to pay the debt for our sins. Here again, we need to reference Hebrews 7:25-27.

"**Just think** – the One, who knew no Sin, took the Sin of all humanity and nailed it to His Cross, that through Him we might have Everlasting Life."

"As Jesus Died Upon the Cross . . ."

Matthew 27:45-46, *"Now from the sixth hour until the ninth hour there was darkness over all the land. And about the ninth hour Jesus cried out with a loud voice, saying, 'Eli, Eli, lama sabachthami?'* That is, "My God, My God, why have You forsaken Me?" Verses 50-51, *"And Jesus cried out again with a loud voice, and yielded up His spirit. Then, behold, the veil of the temple was torn in two from the top to the bottom; and the earth quaked ..."*

Because of Christ's obedience unto death, so that we might live, it is only fitting for us to be obedient unto the Godhead. Obedience to God proves our love for Him (1John 5:2-3), it also demonstrates our faithfulness to Him (1 John 2:3-6), and glorifies Him in this world (1 Peter 2:12). We are to obey our parents, as well as our Heavenly Father. Psalms 128:1 says, *"Blessed is everyone who fears the Lord, who walks in His ways."* God is gracious. If we ask God for forgiveness, because we've been living in and for the world, we can be transformed by His shed blood and He will forget our sin as if we had never committed it in the first place. Hebrews 10:16-17 says, *"This is the covenant that I will make with them after those days, says the Lord: I will put My laws into their hearts, and in their minds I will write them," then He adds, "Their sins and their lawless deeds I will remember no more."*

Questions for Personal Evaluation or Group Discussion

Chapter 12

1. How do our choices differ from God's ways?

2. What are some good choices we should make?

3. Is it possible for good people to go to Hell?

4. What is meant in the Gospel of Luke (prior to the crucifixion) when Jesus Christ prayed in the garden of Gethsemane, and Luke, the physician, mentioned, "His sweat became like great drops of blood falling down to the ground?"

Notes

"A Special Closing Message"

After reading this book, it is our prayer that if you do not know Jesus Christ as your Savior, you will simply understand no matter where you are in terms of a physical location -- you will simply realize that Jesus says "COME". Secondly, He says, "If anyone opens the door of his heart." Next, realize the Bible is clear; we are saved by grace through faith. Abraham believed, and it was credited to him as righteousness. Salvation is a divine work. We are not saved because we respond – We are saved because the Holy Spirit has regenerated our hearts. Repentance is an action – change in direction, in heart and in mind. Read your Bible and pray daily.

You should begin looking for a truly solid Biblical church that is grounded in the Word of God. Do not look for the following signs to finding a good church. A full parking lot, a long list of activities, what the exterior of the church looks like, or a large mega-church, but look for the pure Gospel. Charles Swindoll once said that "If there is a mist behind the pulpit, there is a fog in the pew." The teachings must be clear and concise, they must be easily understood, and they must be expository. Expository preaching is preaching that sheds light on Scriptures and goes through Bible verses or a verse in particular. It makes the text easily understood and does not make the text unnecessarily complex. The gospel has been said to be so simple that a child could wade through it yet so deep that an elephant could swim in it.

__Note:__ Included is an example of a Declaration of Faith / Doctrinal Statement that will assist you in finding a doctrinally sound church.

Also, ask God to direct you to such and do not be afraid to drive or make multiple calls and speak with pastors, at length.

Declaration of Faith / Doctrinal Statement

1. We believe in the verbal inspiration, inerrancy and absolute and final authority of the Scriptures as originally given. We believe God has preserved His Word through all generations and that the Word remains pure and inerrant yet today in those 66 books of the Old and New Testament, and that they are the completed revelation of God for us today (Luke 24:27,44; 2 Timothy 3:16-17, 2 Peter 1:19-21).
2. We believe in the Trinity of the Godhead; that God exists eternally in three divine Persons: God the Father, Son and Holy Spirit (Genesis 1:26; Matthew 28:18-19; 2 Corinthians 13:14).
3. We believe in the Deity of the Lord Jesus Christ (John 1:1, 2, 14), in His virgin birth (Matthew l:18-21; Luke 1:26-28), His perfect and sinless humanity (Philippians 2:6-8; 2 Corinthians 5:21), His vicarious death through the shedding of His blood for the remission of sins (Ephesians 1:7), His bodily resurrection and ascension (1 Corinthians 15:3-4; Acts 1:11), His present high priestly ministry (Hebrews 2:17-18; 4:14-16), and in the imminence of His literal pre-tribulation, and pre-millennial return (Matthew 25:31-46; 1 Thessalonians 4:13-18).
4. We believe in the personality and Deity of the Holy Spirit (John 14:16-17, 26; John 16:13; Romans 8:26-27).
5. We believe in the reality and personality of Satan (Isaiah 14:12-15; 1 Peter 5:8; Revelation 12:9-11).
6. We believe in the fall of man through the sin of Adam (Genesis 3:1-6), and in the consequent necessity of the New Birth through Jesus Christ (John 1:12, 3:3-7).
7. We believe that the salvation of sinners is wholly of grace through faith in the Lord Jesus Christ, in the virtue of His redemptive work on the Cross, and that neither baptism, the

Lord's Supper, nor any other rite, ceremony, nor work can avail one whit for the sinner's salvation. Christ alone saves (Ephesians 2:8-9; Titus 3:5; 1 Peter 1:18-19).

8. We believe that the invisible church, or body of Christ, includes all regenerated persons from Pentecost to the Rapture of the Church, and that her supreme mission is her world-wide commission as set forth by Christ and His Apostles (Acts 2:42-47; 1 Corinthians 12:12-27; Ephesians 1:20-23).
9. We believe that a visible or local church is composed only of Scripturally baptized believers, meeting together as Scripture so commands, with New Testament officers and order (Acts 2:41-42; 1 Corinthians 11:2; Hebrews 10:25).
10. We believe that every human being has direct relations with God and is responsible to God alone in all matters of faith (Matthew 10:28; 23:10); that each church is independent and autonomous and must be free from interference by any ecclesiastical or political authority (Matthew 22:21), and that church and state must be kept separate as having functions each fulfilling its duties free from dictation or patronage of the other (Titus 3:1; Romans 13:1-7).
11. We believe that Christian baptism is the immersion in water of a believer, in the name of the Father, and of the Son, and of the Holy Spirit, in express obedience to the command of the command of our Lord Jesus Christ (Matthew 28:19-20; Acts 8:12, 36-38; 18:8).
12. We believe that the Lord's Supper was established as a means of showing forth in symbol Christ's death for us until He comes and that the Lord's Table should be open to all regenerated persons living in fellowship with, and obedience to the clear commands of Jesus Christ (Luke 22:19-20; 1 Corinthians 11:23-32).
13. We believe in the literal resurrection of the body (John 5:28-29), in the eternal salvation of the regenerate (John 10:28-29; Romans 8:38-39), in the eternal condemnation of the unregenerate (Revelation 20:11-15), in the endless bliss of the

believers (2 Corinthians 5:8; Philippians 1:23, 3:21) and the endless suffering of unbelievers (Revelation 21:8).

14. We believe in the administration of spiritual gifts through the operation of the Holy Spirit; and, that the gifts of evangelists, pastors and teachers are sufficient for the perfecting of the saints today; and, that speaking in tongues and the sign miracles gradually ceased as the New Testament Scriptures were completed and their authority became established. But God, being sovereign in the bestowment of all His gifts, does hear and answer the prayer of faith, in accord with His will, for the sick and afflicted (John 15:7; 1 Corinthians 12:4-11, 13:8-10, 14:21-22; Ephesians 4:11-12; 1 John 5:14-15).
15. We believe in the sanctity of marriage which being sanctioned and defined by God in Scripture joins one man and one woman in a single, permanent, exclusive union (Genesis 2:18-25; Mark 10:6-9; Luke 16:18; Romans 7:2-3; 1 Corinthians 7:1-17). We believe that God intends sexual intimacy to occur between a man and a woman who are married to each other and that all sexual intimacy outside of a marriage between a man and a woman is sin (Hebrews 13:4).
16. We believe that any form of sexual immorality such as adultery, fornication, homosexuality, bisexual conduct, bestiality, incest, pornography or any attempt to alter one's naturally-born gender by surgery or appearance is sinful and offensive to God (Genesis 19:1-13; Leviticus 18:20-22; 1 Corinthians 6:9-11). Accordingly, the church, its pastors, staff and members will not participate in nor condone same sex unions or same sex marriages or anything contrary to our Biblical stance on marriage previously stated, nor shall its property or resources be used for such purposes. Therefore, every adult, child, or youth above the age of 5 must use the bathroom facility that matches the gender on their birth certificate.

Closing Note: Should you have questions concerning the previous material in this book, please reference the Bible (Basic Instructions before Leaving Earth). We believe God to be the final authority.

* * *

God's Sovereignty – Beginning Without End

"...My Counsel shall stand, and I will do
All My Pleasure." (Isaiah 46:8-11)

Recommended Resources

A Shepherd Looks at the 23rd Psalm (Phillip Keller)

A Woman Rides the Beast by Dave Hunt

A.W. Tozer

Bible Answers for Every Need by Clarence L. Blasier

In Defense of the Faith by Dave Hunt

Lighthouse Trails Publishing

Positive Action Bible Curriculum

Proverbs (Bible Study) by Warren Wiersbe

The Berean Call (Dave Hunt & T.A. McMahon)

The Knowledge of the Holy by A.W. Tozer

The Seduction of Christianity by Dave Hunt

The Total Money Makeover by Dave Ramsey

Twelve Ordinary Men by John MacArthur

Through the Bible Commentary by J. Vernon McGee

What Love is This? By Dave Hunt

The Bible Alphabet Sentence

A Bible consistently deals effectively, fervently, generously, heavenly, intelligently, justifiably, Kindly, lovingly, meaningfully, notably, optimistically, peacefully, quantifiably, responsibly, securely, totally, universally, victoriously, wonderfully, xrayable, yieldingly, and zealously to grow a good life.

– LaMarr Pirkle

[Appendix]

Scripture for Needs

Repentance:

Acts 3:19
Luke 13:3
Mark 1:14-15

Forgiving Others:

Ephesians 4:32
Romans 12:21
1 Peter 3:8-9
Mark 11:25-26

Faith:

Hebrews 11:1
Romans 10:17
Mark 9:23
Romans 5:1-2
2 Corinthians 5:7

Fear:

2 Timothy 1:7
John 14:27
Psalm 27:1

Forgiveness of Sins:

1 John 1:9
Psalm 103:12
Matthew 26:28
2 Chronicles 7:14

Temptation:

James 1:12-14
Ephesians 6:11
1 Peter 5:8-9
James 4:7
1 Corinthians 10:13

Printed in the United States
By Bookmasters